普通高等教育教材

# 民航实用英语

李 姝　姚晓鸣　主　编
陈 妍　李 斐　吴立杰　副主编

**Practical English for Civil Aviation**

化学工业出版社
·北京·

## 内容简介

《民航实用英语（下册）》共6个单元，旨在通过真实浓厚的行业背景、身临其境的职业场景、原汁原味的客舱用语、实用丰富的民航知识和有针对性的练习来提高学生英语交际能力和客舱服务水平。主要内容包括：医疗服务和急救、特殊乘客服务、应急救援、免税购物、着陆服务事宜和海关检查。

本书可供本科院校航空服务艺术与管理专业、高职高专院校空中乘务专业英语教学使用，也可作为航空公司新引进乘务人员的英语培训教材，或成熟乘务人员复训时英语书面及口语测试的参考材料。

### 图书在版编目（CIP）数据

民航实用英语．下册/李姝，姚晓鸣主编．—北京：化学工业出版社，2023.2
普通高等教育教材
ISBN 978-7-122-42585-0

Ⅰ．①民… Ⅱ．①李… ②姚… Ⅲ．①民用航空-英语-高等学校-教材 Ⅳ．①F56

中国版本图书馆CIP数据核字（2022）第229019号

---

责任编辑：旷英姿　姜　磊　　　　　　　　文字编辑：李　曦
责任校对：赵懿桐　　　　　　　　　　　　装帧设计：王晓宇

---

出版发行：化学工业出版社（北京市东城区青年湖南街13号　邮政编码100011）
印　　装：三河市延风印装有限公司
787mm×1092mm　1/16　印张7¾　字数176千字　2023年8月北京第1版第1次印刷

购书咨询：010-64518888　　　　　　　　　售后服务：010-64518899
网　　址：http://www.cip.com.cn
凡购买本书，如有缺损质量问题，本社销售中心负责调换。

定　　价：26.00元　　　　　　　　　　　　　　　　　　版权所有　违者必究

# 前言
## PREFACE

以习近平总书记在全国教育大会上的讲话精神为引领，围绕新时代民航强国战略，以培养具有鲜明民航特色和文化基因的高素质国际化、专业化人才为导向，根据民航业空中乘务员实际工作需求，参照《教育部关于全面提高高等教育质量的若干意见》的精神，践行《高等学校课程思政建设指导纲要》，我们组织全国多所高校和民航企业设计、编写了这套《民航实用英语（上、下）》。本套教材将价值塑造、知识传授和能力培养三者融为一体，旨在通过真实浓厚的行业背景、身临其境的职业场景、原汁原味的客舱用语、实用丰富的民航知识和有针对性的练习来提高学生英语交际能力和客舱服务水平。

一、教材编写理念与特色

教材编写体现以下理念与特色：

➢ 学生为本重参与

教材聚焦语言知识，注重学生语言技能和思维能力的培养，以"微对话、微知识、微任务"激发学生的学习兴趣，通过活动及练习的设置引导学生在"做"中"学"，在真实的语言交际环境中掌握使用英语应对空乘服务中的各类常规服务、特殊服务及个性化服务的能力。

➢ 能力体系多维度

教材注重全面培养学生的英语听、说、读、写、译能力，提高学生科学人文素养，并培养他们以英语为媒介从事专业学习和跨文化交际的能力。以空乘服务的基本流程为主线，融合知识点、文化视点和案例分析，延展了专业知识学习的广度与深度，培养国际化人才。

➢ 教材资源立体化

创建基于二维码扫描的教学课件资源、听力音频资源和课程学习拓展资源，融纸质教材与数字资源为一体，发挥移动学习的特点和优势，把学生思维能力、创新能力和审美能力的培养有机地融入教材的编写中去。

➢ 拓展训练强能力

创建理想环境，使学生在真实的语境中把单元所学知识和技能用于实际任务，以内化语言知识、巩固学习技能，培养其创新意识、解决问题和团队协作能力。

➢ 立德树人全过程

教材在编写中融入课程思政元素，落实立德树人根本任务，体现社会主义核心价值观。每单元设有名言名句，呼应和拓展单元情境，提炼思政主题。在教学过程中进行多样化探索，通过线下情境式教学、线上延展式教学等多种方式实现教学目标，达到学以致用、知行合一。

## 二、教材单元结构

本套教材由上、下两册组成，根据航空服务基本流程共设计了12个单元。其中上册包含 Ticketing, Baggage Handling, Security Checks, Boarding Service, Pre-flight Service, In-flight Service 六个单元；下册包含 Medical Service and First Aid, Special Passenger Service, Emergency Procedures, Duty Free Shopping, Landing, Customs Check 六个单元。单元结构如下：

### 1. Learning Objectives

明确单元"价值塑造、知识传授和能力培养"三位一体育人目标，提升学生人文素质和民航英语应用能力。

### 2. Language Skills

聚焦民航英语真实情境中的语言策略与技能，提高学生学习质效。

① Lead-in

导入短文意蕴深远，名人名言隽永绵长，激发学生学习兴趣与思考，引入本单元主题。

② Listening as Comprehension

结合两则对话或通知开展听力练习，侧重听写技能训练。

③ Reading as Acquisition

阅读两篇主题相关文章，帮助学生掌握客舱服务的基本知识和英语表述。此部分设有文化视点（Culture Notes），提高学生对文章的理解和跨文化交际能力。

④ Speaking for Communication

结合单元主题，模仿真实语境对话开展口语活动，培养学生的英语运用能力。

⑤ Case Study

案例分析帮助学生提升对突发事件的应急处理能力。

⑥ Further Practice

学生以小组或结对形式完成写作、翻译和口语等练习，帮助学生巩固所学知识，发展综合能力。

## 三、教材适用范围

本书可供本科院校航空服务艺术与管理专业、高职高专院校空中乘务专业英语教学使用，也可作为航空公司新引进乘务人员英语培训教材，或成熟乘务人员复训时英语书面及口语测试的参考材料。

本套教材下册由沈阳师范大学李姝、中原工学院姚晓鸣主编，沈阳师范大学陈妍、江苏旅游职业学院李斐、沈阳航空航天大学吴立杰副主编，江苏旅游职业学院李庆参加编写。在编写过程中，参考了国内外相关文献，在此表示由衷的感谢！

由于编者水平所限，教材中难免有疏漏与不足，恳请各位专家、教师和同学们批评指正。

编者
2022年11月

# 目录 CONTENTS

Unit One　Medical Service and First Aid
（医疗服务和急救） … 1

Unit Two　Special Passenger Service
（特殊乘客服务） … 16

Unit Three　Emergency Procedures
（应急救援） … 30

Unit Four　Duty-free Shopping
（免税购物） … 44

Unit Five　Landing
（着陆服务事宜） … 57

Unit Six　Customs Check
（海关检查） … 72

Appendix（附录） … 90

Appendix 1
　Glossary List 词汇表　90

Appendix 2
　Listening Script 听力原文　98

Answer Keys（参考答案） … 103

References（参考文献） … 116

# Unit One　Medical Service and First Aid
（医疗服务和急救）

Unit One

After learning, you will be able to:

1. Master the key language points and useful expressions about Medical Service and First Aid;

2. Understand airsickness and first aids in flight;

3. Work in teams to find out solutions to problems you might meet in flight;

4. Conduct a series of writing, reading, speaking and translating activities related to the theme of the Unit.

## Part One　Lead-in: Calmness

**Directions:** Calmness is one of the qualities that flight attendants should have to possess. After reading a short passage about calmness you may have a deeper understanding of the two quotations from Dickens and Confucius respectively, which will guide you to be better adapted to the demanding work place.

# Calmness: Why It's an Important Quality for a Flight Attendant

For various reasons, passengers may suffer from illness, shock, or even death on board. Therefore, the flight attendants shall have the necessary medical knowledge to calmly deal with the actual conditions of passengers for effective treatment, seek help of doctors on board when necessary, get in contact with the ground to arrange the ambulance and medical personnel, and make every effort to protect and save the life safety of the passengers.

Now discuss with your partner about your understanding of the following two quotations. Please take experience of yourself or others for examples to support your argument.

无论做什么事情，都不要着急。不管发生什么事，都要冷静、沉着。

——查尔斯·狄更斯

No matter what you do, don't worry. No matter what happens, be calm and calm.

——Charles Dickens

三思而后行。

——孔子

Look before you leap.

——Confucius

## Part Two   Listening as Comprehension

**Directions:** Listen to the following two announcements and fill in the blanks according to what you hear, then create an announcement based on the substitutions given and speak it out.

# Announcement A

## Introduction to Cabin Equipment and Airsickness

Ladies and gentlemen,

　　Welcome 1) _____ China Eastern Airlines Flight MU5109 from Shanghai to Beijing. The distance is about 1100 kilometers. Our flight will take two hours and twenty minutes. Breakfast has been prepared for you. We will 2) _____ you before we serve it.

　　Now, I will tell you where the cabin 3) _____ locates and how to use them. Your seat-back can be reclined by pressing the recliner button on your armrest. The reading light, 4) _____ and air vent are located above your seat. Airsickness bags are in the seat pocket in front of you.

　　If you feel like vomiting, please use it. If you are 5) _____ and need some airsick tablets, you can press the call button to 6) _____ us.

　　Lavatories are located in the front and rear of the cabin. 7) _____ is strictly prohibited on board.

　　We wish you a 8) _____ flight.

　　Thank you!

## Words and Expressions

cabin [ˈkæbɪn] *n.* 机舱
equipment [ɪˈkwɪpmənt] *n.* 设备
recline [rɪˈklaɪn] *v.* 向后倾斜
armrest [ˈɑːmrest] *n.* 扶手
air vent 通风口
airsickness [ˈeəsɪknəs] *n.* 晕机
vomit [ˈvɒmɪt] *v.* 呕吐
lavatory [ˈlævətri] *n.* 厕所，盥洗室
prohibit [prəˈhɪbɪt] *v.* 禁止

# Speaking A

**Directions:** Imitate the above announcement to make an announcement according to the following substitution.

## Substitution

1. Welcome aboard { China Southern Airlines / Hainan Airlines / Xiamen Airlines } Flight

{ CZ8882 from Shanghai to Tianjin.  
HU7614 from Hainan to Shanghai.  
MF8556 from Xiamen to Chengdu. } The distance is about { 1100  
670  
1900 }

kilometers. Our flight will take { two hours.  
one hour and ten minutes.  
two hours and twenty minutes. }

2. { Breakfast  
Lunch  
Dinner } has been prepared for you.

3. If you { suffer from airsickness,  
feel like vomiting,  
feel pains in your ears, } please { take some tablets for it.  
use airsickness bags.  
chew a gum or a candy.  
sit still and have a rest. }

4. If you are { airsick  
earache  
headache } and need { some airsick tablets,  
a free chewing gum,  
a hot towel, }

you can press the call button to contact us.

5. We wish you a(n) { pleasant  
enjoyable  
comfortable } flight.

## Announcement B

### Searching for a Doctor and Making an Emergency Landing

Ladies and gentlemen,

May I have your 1) _____ , please?

We have a passenger 2) _____ on our aircraft. If you are a 3) _____, we would appreciate your assistance by 4) _____ our flight attendants as soon as possible.

Due to the serious condition of the passenger, the captain has decided to make an emergency 5) _____ at Beijing Capital International Airport. We expect

Announcement B

to arrive there in two hours and twenty-nine minutes.

We 6) _____ for any inconvenience. Thank you for your 7) _____ and 8) _____ !

## Words and Expressions

aircraft [ˈeəkrɑːft] *n.* 飞机
appreciate [əˈpriːʃieɪt] *v.* 感激
assistance [əˈsɪstəns] *n.* 帮助
emergency landing 紧急迫降
apologize [əˈpɒlədʒaɪz] *v.* 道歉
inconvenience [ˌɪnkənˈviːniəns] *n.* 不方便

## Speaking B

**Directions:** Imitate the above announcement to make an announcement according to the following substitution.

### Substitution

1. We have a passenger { in shock / in need of medical treatment / suffering a heart attack } on our aircraft.

2. If you are { a doctor, / a nurse, / a physician, } we would appreciate your assistance by { informing / contacting / identifying yourself to } our flight attendants as soon as possible.

3. Due to the serious condition of the passenger, the captain has decided to make an emergency landing at { Beijing Daxing International Airport. / Guangzhou Baiyun International Airport. / Haikou Meilan International Airport. }

4. We expect to arrive there in { thirty minutes. / one hour and ten minutes. }

# Part Three  Reading as Acquisition

## Text A

### What Is Airsickness?

Nausea is one common symptom of airsickness.

Airsickness is a form of motion sickness experienced by some air travelers. It is caused by a disruption in the body's balance. Nausea, headaches, fatigue, paleness, dizziness and vomiting are some of the body's reactions to airsickness.

Trying to prevent air travel sickness is important because once the symptoms begin, they usually do not cease until the airplane has landed and stopped moving. There are several strategies for preventing airsickness. Sitting in the front of the airplane or in locations that experience less movement, such as near the wings, is usually helpful. It is also important to make sure there is adequate ventilation directed at the face through the use of airplane air vents. Eating lighter meals and avoiding fatty meals prior to travel can help decrease the symptoms of nausea.

Passengers can take medicines to prevent or reduce these uncomfortable symptoms. These medicines are usually to be taken prior to travel. The symptoms usually disappear completely once the motion has stopped. Once the passengers have the airsick symptoms, flight attendants should take the initiative to care and help, placate in patience and provide a few more cleaning bags, hot towels and warm boiling water, to smooth them over.

The effects of air travel sickness are temporary but annoying for individuals who need to travel for a living. Pilots and flight attendants, for example, need to deal with the problem in order to sustain long-term careers. Studies show that relaxation and breathing techniques have helped many of these individuals to overcome this problem. In general, as individuals are used to flying, their incidences of airsickness decrease.

### Decide whether the statements are true or false according to the passage.

1. Passengers who are airsick may have many symptoms, such as headache, dizziness, vomiting, etc.

(    )

2. Strategies such as sitting in the front or rear of the plane are very helpful for passengers to prevent airsickness.

(    )

3. Passengers suffering airsickness cannot eat anything.    (    )

4. It's more effective for passengers to take medicine to prevent or reduce airsickness before boarding.

(    )

5. Pilots and flight attendants who suffer from airsickness cannot overcome this problem.
(　　)

## Words and Expressions

disruption [dɪsˈrʌpʃn] *n.* 妨碍；扰乱
nausea [ˈnɔːziə] *n.* 恶心
symptom [ˈsɪmptəm] *n.* 症状
ventilation [ˌventɪˈleɪʃn] *n.* 通风
prior [ˈpraɪə(r)] *adj.* 事先的
placate [pləˈkeɪt] *v.* 安抚
temporary [ˈtemprəri] *adj.* 暂时的

### 如何避免和缓解晕机症状

　　晕机和晕车、晕船等一样，医学上统称为运动病。晕机症状因人而异，有轻重之分。轻者表现为头晕，全身稍有不适、胸闷、脸色绯红。重者则脸色青白、头痛心慌、微汗。更严重的会出现浑身盗汗、眩晕恶心、呕吐不止等难以忍受的痛苦。造成晕机的因素很多，有飞机颠簸、起飞、爬高、下降、着陆、转弯，或乘客心情紧张、身体不适、过度疲劳等。

　　一般健康者和有轻微晕机的人，坐MD82以上的现代化、大型客机，都不会发生晕机。严重晕机的乘客，若能采取以下预防措施可以避免或减轻晕机症状。

1. 乘机的前一天晚上，充足地睡眠休息，保证第二天乘机有充沛的精力。
2. 应在飞机起飞前1小时，至少也要提前半小时口服晕机宁。
3. 尽量挑选距发动机较远又靠近窗的座位，能减少噪音和扩大视野。
4. 在空中应多做一些精力集中的事和活动。如看书、聊天、听音乐等。
5. 保持空间定向是十分重要的。视线要尽量放远，看远处的云和山脉、河，不要看近处的云。
6. 一旦发生晕机，如果症状较轻，保持空间定向，视线尽量放远，不看近处。如果较重，应该安静、坐稳，最好是仰卧、固定头部。
7. 防止条件反射。发现周围旅客有迹象要呕吐应立即离开现场，避开视线。

## Text B

## First Aid

First aid is emergency care for a victim of sudden illness or injury until more skillful medical treatment is available. First aid may save a life or improve certain vital signs including pulse, temperature, an unobstructed airway, and breathing. In minor emergencies, first aid may prevent a victim's condition from worsening and provide relief from pain. First aid must be administered as quickly as possible. In the case of the critically injured, a few minutes can make the difference between complete recovery and loss of life.

During the flight, medical problems may often occur. If the passenger suffers from a serious condition, the plane will make an emergency landing at an alternate airport and ask for emergency help to be waiting for them on arrival. If it is not a life-threatening condition, the crew, especially the cabin attendants can often handle it without difficulty. Therefore, first aid is essential knowledge for the cabin attendants.

First-aid measures depend upon a victim's needs and provider's level of knowledge and skill. Knowing what not to do in an emergency is as important as knowing what to do. Improperly moving a person with a neck injury, for example, can lead to permanent spinal injury and paralysis.

Despite the variety of injuries possible, several principles of first aid apply to all emergencies. The first step is to call for professional medical help. The victim, if conscious, should be reassured that medical aid has been requested, and asked for permission to provide any first aid. Next, assess the scene, asking other people or the injured person's family or friends about details of the injury or illness, any care that may have already been given, and preexisting conditions such as diabetes or heart trouble. The victim should be checked for medical bracelet or card that describes special medical conditions. Unless the accident scene becomes unsafe or the victim may suffer further injury, do not move the victim.

First aid requires rapid assessment of victims to determine whether life-threatening conditions exist. One method for evaluating a victim's condition is known as the ABC, which stands for:

A—Airway: is it open and unobstructed?

B—Breathing: is the person breathing? Look, listen, and feel for her/his breathing.

C—Circulation: is there a pulse? Is the person bleeding externally? Check skin color and temperature for additional indications of circulation problem.

Once obvious injuries have been evaluated, the injured person's head should be kept in a neutral position in line with the body. If no evidence exists to suggest potential skull or spinal injury, place the injured person in a comfortable position. Positioned on one side, a victim can vomit without choking or obstructing the airway.

## The following questions are based on the passage and choose the best answer.

1. It is very important in first aid to _____.

A. move the injured person from the scene of accident immediately

B. spend a few minutes for making the difference between recovery and death

C. know what to do and what not to do according to the condition of the victim

D. remove the medical bracelet or card from the victim

2. One of the following practices is NOT right in the first aid, that is _____.

A. to check whether the victim is breathing

B. to let the victim lie on one side

C. to telephone a hospital at once

D. to wait patiently for more skillful medical treatment before carrying on first aid

3. The article implies that the provider of first aid should be especially careful _____.

A. in handing the victim only if he or she learns that the victim has both diabetes and heart trouble

B. in handing the victim if he or she learns that the victim has diabetes or heart trouble

C. not to move the victim if he or she finds a medical bracelet on the victim

D. not to move the victim if he or she finds the accident scene to be unsafe

4. According to this article, first aid is usually provided by _____.

A. professional doctors

B. the victim's family members

C. the victim's friends

D. those people who are not necessarily professional doctors

5. This article can be said to be one to _____.

A. give basic knowledge about how to practice first aid

B. give a brief introduction to the history of first aid

C. give some knowledge to anyone who may be injured in an accident

D. give warning that first aid is dangerous to those who do not know how to deal with it

## Words and Expressions

victim [ˈvɪktɪm] *n.* 受害者，患病者

unobstructed [ˌʌnəbˈstrʌktɪd] *adj.* 没有障碍的，畅通无阻的

airway [ˈeəweɪ] *n.* 呼吸道

administer [ədˈmɪnɪstə(r)] *v.* 实施

life-threatening [ˈlaɪf θretnɪŋ] *adj.* 威胁生命的

spinal [ˈspaɪnl] *adj.* 脊柱的

paralysis [pəˈræləsɪs] *n.* 瘫痪

conscious [ˈkɒnʃəs] *adj.* 神志清醒的

assessment [əˈsesmənt] *n.* 评估

circulation [ˌsɜːkjəˈleɪʃn] *n.* 血液循环

## Culture Notes

### 急救箱

在旅途中，很多人会由于生病而突然眩晕等。因此，应急医疗设备成为挽救人们生命的关键。急救箱是发生意外伤害事件时非常重要也非常有用的一件物品，但你知道急救箱里都有什么东西吗？现在就让我们看看吧：急救箱中有绷带（bandage）、止血带、三角巾（triangular bandage）、剪刀、钳子、棉签（alcohol-dampened wipes）、酒精棉（alcohol prep pads）、创可贴（band-aid）、冰袋（ice pack）、手电筒（torch）和药品。

绷带可包扎伤口和身体受伤部位；止血带仅用于包扎在受伤的手臂或大腿上，防止大出血；三角巾是一种急救绷带，可承托受伤的上肢、固定辅料或者骨折处；剪刀和钳子可用来剪开胶布或绷带；棉签可用来清洁伤口；酒精棉用来消毒；创可贴贴在皮肤上以覆盖伤口特别是小伤口；装满冰的冰袋置于瘀伤、肌肉拉伤或关节扭伤的部位，令微血管收缩，可帮助减少肿胀；在漆黑环境下施救时，可用手电筒照明。

## Part Four  Speaking for Communication

**Directions:** Act out the conversations with your partners.

### Conversation A  Airsickness

（CC=Cabin Crew, P=Passenger）

CC: Are you all right, Madam? You look pale. What can I do for you?

P: I'm not feeling very well.

CC: What's your symptoms?

P: I feel dizzy. What's more, I feel like vomiting.

CC: You might be airsick. Have you ever suffered airsickness before?

P: Oh, no. This is my first time to take the plane. What should I do?

CC: Don't worry. You'd better sit still and have a rest in order to relieve the symptoms.

Conversation A

And I'll get you some medicine for airsickness.

(A minute later)

CC: Here's the medicine and a glass of water.

P: Thank you.

CC: You may find an airsick bag in the pocket of the seat in front of you. If you still feel sick, you may use it. And you can also use this hot towel to wipe your face, which would make you feel better.

P: All right. You are so considerate.

CC: If you have any requirement, please call us immediately.

P: Thank you so much.

CC: You are welcome, madam.

## Words and Expressions

dizzy [ˈdɪzi] *adj.* 眩晕的

towel [ˈtaʊəl] *n.* 毛巾

wipe [waɪp] *v.* 擦拭

considerate [kənˈsɪdərət] *adj.* 体贴的，考虑周到的

requirement [rɪˈkwaɪəmənt] *n.* 要求

## Conversation B    Pains in Ears

(FA=Flight Attendant, P=Passenger)

Conversation B

P: Excuse me, miss. I don't feel very well.

FA: Is there anything wrong, sir?

P: The earache is killing me! Could you please help me with that?

FA: Oh, I'm sorry to hear that! Don't worry, sir. Is this the first time you travel by plane?

P: Yes.

FA: That's right. The pain in your ears is due to a change in air pressure. The symptom is common during the flight, especially for the people who don't often take the plane.

P: What should I do to relieve my symptom?

FA: You can relieve the earache by swallowing or chewing gums.

(Five minutes later, the passenger presses the button once again.)

FA: How do you feel now?

P: I've even had two pieces of chewing gums in my mouth, but it did not work at all. Oh, my god, what serious earache it is!

FA: Well, let me tell you another way to relieve your earache. Firstly you can draw a deep breath, then stop your nose with the fingers and try to blow your nose. Like this, how are you feeling now?

P: Oh, yeah, it seems effective. Thank you very much.

FA: You're welcome.

## Words and Expressions

earache [ˈɪəreɪk] *n.* 耳痛

air pressure 气压

relieve [rɪˈliːv] *v.* 缓解（疼痛或不快的感觉）

swallow [ˈswɒləʊ] *v.* 吞咽
chew [tʃuː] *v.* 咀嚼
blow [bləʊ] *v.* 擤（鼻子）
effective [ɪˈfektɪv] *adj.* 有效的

## Part Five   Case Study

案例一：某航班上，乘务员在巡视的过程中发现一位外国老太太头靠在座椅上，眼睛呆滞地望向前方。乘务员赶紧上前询问，发现老人没有任何反应，此时，老人已经昏迷、不省人事。若你是该乘务员，请问应该如何处理？

案例二：在某航班快要接近目的地时，一名坐在客舱后半段的72岁老人突发心脏病！这并不是航班上第一次遇到这样的情况，但与之前几次不同的是，这次犯病的老人在吃下随身携带的药物后没有缓解，最坏的结果随时可能出现。若你是机上乘务员，请问应该如何处理？

## Part Six   Further Practice

### Task 1   Writing

**Directions**: Write an announcement that goes when searching for doctors by using the following words or expressions:

medical attention, doctor/physician/medical professional/medically trained person, cabin attendants/flight attendants

Announcement

_____
_____
_____
_____

### Task 2   Translating

**Directions:** Translate the following sentences into English.

1. 放轻松，这种症状很常见。

2. 如果感觉想吐，请使用呕吐袋，就在前方座椅的口袋中。

3. 很抱歉，飞机上没有医生，但我们已经与目的地机场的地面服务人员取得了联系。

4. 您可以通过咀嚼口香糖或吞咽口水来缓解耳痛。

5. 您以前有感觉心脏不舒服吗？您有没有随身携带药物？有同行的人吗？

6. 这是晕机药，这是热毛巾，我建议您把它放在额头上休息一下，您会稍微舒服一些。

7. 抬高手臂，清洗一下伤口。不要紧张，血已经止住了，我用纱布将伤口包扎起来。

8. 机长决定备降最近的机场。

## Task 3  Story Reading and Retelling

**Directions:** Read the following story in a group and retell it to your group members in your own words.

A flight attendant has recalled a rare experience of assisting in the transfer of a badly injured boy from Hotan City to Urumqi City in northwest China's Xinjiang Uygur Autonomous Region.

Zhao Yan, chief stewardess on the flight between Hotan and Urumqi, said that the captain notified her that he was taking the plane back to the terminal as it was poised for takeoff late on April 30.

An anxious father had arrived at the airport pleading for help as the time approached midnight and the last flight of the day to the regional capital Urumqi – the one Zhao was on – was about to depart.

The man's seven-year-old son had wounded his arm in a tractor accident and was in urgent need of surgery in Urumqi. It didn't take long before the airline and relevant authorities approved the request and asked the plane to turn around to pick up the new passengers.

In an interview with a news website affiliated to the Ministry of Transport of the People's Republic of China, Zhao said she worried the passengers would complain about the delay before breaking the news to them. But none raised an objection.

The cabin crew set up a special space for the injured boy on the plane and later donated money to help the family. As the doctors said the boy shouldn't fall asleep throughout the journey, Zhao helped keep him awake by playing music and using ice cubes to cool the severed limb.

During the flight, some passengers also helped take care of the boy, she recalled.

About 90 minutes later, the plane landed at the airport in Urumqi, where a medical team was waiting to take the boy to hospital.

A string of green channels with a police car leading the way helped make the transfer fast and smooth.

The operation took about three and a half hours early morning on May 1 and the severed arm was reattached.

"Thanks a million. Our family owes so much to everyone involved in the relay race," said the boy's father, who preferred to stay anonymous.

"We just had a special Labor Day," Li Li, one of the surgeons who performed the operation, said on his WeChat account.

"Everyone was racing against time to help retain the seven-year-old Uygur's arm," Li said.

## Task 4  Situational Conversation

**Directions:** The subject matters are given below for several kinds of conversations between the flight attendants and the passengers. Make up short dialogues—four or five lines—that could develop from these situations. Act out the conversation with your partners.

1. An old passenger is running a fever. The flight attendant comes to ask if he needs any help.

2. It is the first time for Mr. Li to travel by plane. He doesn't feel very well in his ears. The flight attendant gives him some advice.

3. Mary, the flight attendant, is patrolling the cabin. She finds that a passenger looks pale. After simple communication, she knows that the passenger is suffering from airsickness. Then she provides the passenger some medicine, a wet towel and some hot water to relieve his/her symptoms.

4. A passenger has a stomachache and he/she asks help from the flight attendant.

5. A passenger's finger is cut by the rough edge of the chair, and the flight attendant helps bandage the wound.

| Commonly Used English for Medical Care and First Aids | |
|---|---|
| Inquiring about passengers | You look pale. What's wrong with you? |
| | Are you feeling sick or having a headache? |
| | How long have you been feeling this way? |
| | Is this your first time travelling by plane? |
| Response to inquiries | We are now broadcasting for doctors and nurses. |
| | Sorry, but there is no doctor here on the plane. |
| Giving suggestions | You can relieve your earache by chewing a gum or a candy. |
| | You'd better sit still and have a rest in order to relieve the symptoms. |
| | You may feel better if you chew a gum. |
| | You may lie down and have a rest. |
| | You may feel better if you wipe your face with the towel. |
| Asking for permission | May I take your temperature? |
| | Shall I bring you some hot water? |
| Explanation | The pain in your ears is due to the change in air pressure. |
| | You may find an airsick bag in the pocket of the seat in front of you. |
| | I think you are suffering from airsickness. |
| | It's quite common. |

| Commonly Used English for Medical Care and First Aids ||
|---|---|
| Inquiring needs | If you are not feeling any better, please call us. |
| | If you need anything, just press the service button on the arm of the seat. |
| Supplying medicine and water | I'll bring you a glass of hot water to help you relax. |
| | I may get you some tablets for airsickness. |
| | Here is the medicine for airsickness and a cup of water. |
| | I'll go and get the first-aid kit. |
| Reassurance | Just relax. |
| | You will be feeling better soon. |
| Bandaging the wound | Please press the wound with gauze. |
| | I'll help you to clean the wound. |
| | I'll bandage your wound. |

# Unit Two    Special Passenger Service
（特殊乘客服务）

Unit Two

After learning, you will be able to:

1. Master the key language points and useful expressions about Special Passenger Service;

2. Understand restrictions to the transportation of pregnant women and rules about pets;

3. Work in teams to find out solutions to problems you might meet in flight;

4. Conduct a series of writing, reading, speaking and translating activities related to the theme of the Unit.

## Part One    Lead-in: Love

**Directions:** Love is one of the qualities that flight attendants should have. After reading a short passage about love you may have a deeper understanding of the two quotations from Gorky and Tolstoy respectively, which will guide you to be better adapted to the demanding work place.

# Love: Why It's an Important Quality for a Flight Attendant

Love is kindness to travelers. Service is interpersonal communication. High-quality service is pleasant interpersonal communication, the resonance of beautiful emotions between people, and love is the foundation of beautiful emotions. The love of flight attendants to passengers is very important to create a high-quality service atmosphere. As an excellent flight attendant, he/she should first be a kind and caring person, and the service based on love is sincere service. If there is no sincere love, a flight attendant who only relies on skills to serve, will never be possible to truly retain passengers for the airline, and will never be possible to become an excellent flight attendant.

Now discuss with your partner about your understanding of the following two quotations. Please take experience of yourself or others for examples to support your argument.

> 应该尊重彼此间的相互帮助,这在社会生活中是必不可少的。
> ——马克西姆·高尔基
> Mutual help should be respected, which is indispensable in social life.
> ——Maxim Gorky

> 爱和友善便是真实和幸福快乐,并且是全世界真正存有和唯一可能的幸福快乐。
> ——列夫·托尔斯泰
> Love and kindness are truth and happiness, and the only real existence and possible happiness in the world.
> ——Leo Tolstoy

## Part Two    Listening as Comprehension

**Directions**: Listen to the following two announcements and fill in the blanks according to what you hear, then create an announcement based on the substitutions given and speak it out.

### Announcement A

#### Take Care of the Special Passengers

Ladies and gentlemen,

We have just left for Beijing.

Announcement A

During our trip, we shall 1) _____ the service of lunch with beverages. We have prepared 2) _____ for you. This aircraft has audio 3) _____; you can use the earphone to choose what you like.

Our captain is a pilot with rich flying 4) _____. As a result, his perfect flying skills will assure you a safe 5) _____. Meanwhile, our "Amiable Angels" in the cabin, who have rich working experience, will take care of the 6) _____ passengers. To ensure your 7) _____ during the flight, we advise you to fasten your seatbelt while seated. If you have any 8) _____ or requirements, please let us know.

Wish you a pleasant journey!
Thank you!

## Words and Expressions

beverage [ˈbevərɪdʒ] *n.* 饮料
prepare [prɪˈpeə(r)] *v.* 准备
audio [ˈɔːdiəʊ] *adj.* 录音的
captain [ˈkæptɪn] *n.* 机长
assure [əˈʃʊə(r)] *v.* 保证
Amiable Angel 亲情使者
ensure [ɪnˈʃʊə(r)] *v.* 确保
seatbelt [ˈsiːtbelt] *n.* 座位安全带

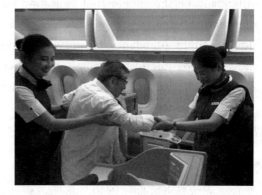

## Speaking A

Speaking A

**Directions:** Imitate the above announcement to make an announcement according to the following substitution.

### Substitution

1. We have just left for { Shanghai. / Shenzhen. / New York. }

2. During our trip, we shall provide the service of { refreshments / meals / snacks / dinner / lunch } with beverages.

3. We have prepared { newspapers / magazines } for you.

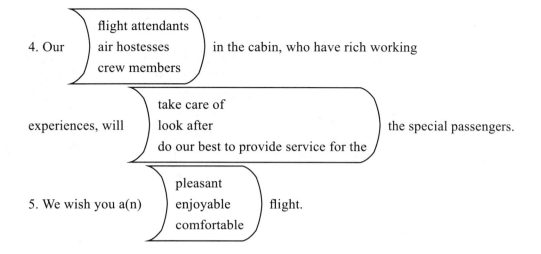

4. Our { flight attendants / air hostesses / crew members } in the cabin, who have rich working experiences, will { take care of / look after / do our best to provide service for the } the special passengers.

5. We wish you a(n) { pleasant / enjoyable / comfortable } flight.

## Announcement B

### Pre-boarding Announcement

Ladies and gentlemen,

　　Good 1）_____.

　　This is the pre-boarding 2）_____ for Flight 4578 to Shanghai. We are now inviting those passengers with small 3）_____ , and any passengers requiring 4）_____ assistance, to begin boarding at this time.

　　Please have your 5）_____ and identification ready. Regular boarding will begin in approximately 6）_____ minutes.

　　Thank you.

## Words and Expressions

pre-boarding announcement 登机前广播
assistance [əˈsɪstəns] *n.* 帮助
boarding pass 登机牌
identification [aɪˌdentɪfɪˈkeɪʃn] *n.* 身份证明
approximately [əˈprɒksɪmətli] *adv.* 大约

## Speaking B

**Directions:** Imitate the above announcement to make an announcement according to the following substitution.

### Substitution

1. { Good morning, / Good afternoon, / Good evening, } passengers.

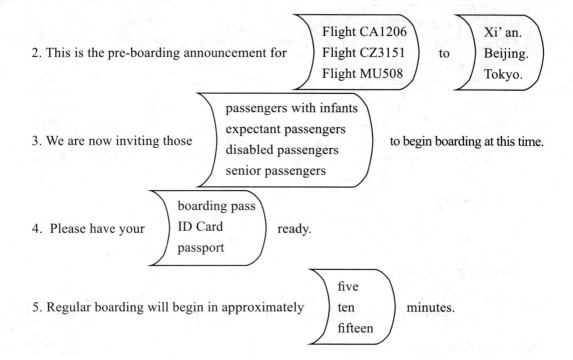

## Part Three   Reading as Acquisition

### Text A

### Pregnant Women

Because oxygen and air pressure decrease in the upper atmosphere, transportation of pregnant women has been restricted to some extent.

Pregnant women whose pregnancy does not exceed 32 weeks (inclusive) can be transported as regular passengers except when the passenger has been advised by her doctor that she is not fit for air travel.

If you are pregnant for over 32 weeks, you are generally not accepted to board the plane. In the case of special circumstances when you are pregnant for more than 32 weeks and less than 36 weeks, you have to file applications to the ticket sales department directly under CS Air before booking tickets and provide diagnosis proof that contains the items as follows:

- Name and age of passenger;
- Date of pregnancy;
- Flights and dates of travel;
- Whether or not they are fit for air travel;
- Whether or not special onboard care is required, etc.

The aforementioned medical diagnostic certificate shall be issued within 72 hours prior to the flight departure and shall be sealed by a hospital, not below the national level and signed by the doctor before validation.

Passengers whose pregnancy exceeds 9 months (36 weeks) and the expected delivery date is within 4 weeks or uncertain, or if it is known that there will be multiple births or delivery complications, will not be accepted for transportation.

## The following questions are based on the passage and choose the best answer:

1. Why do the airlines have restriction to the transportation of pregnant women?_____

A. Because decrease in oxygen and air pressure is not very good for them.

B. Because they may vomit in flight.

C. Because they are not allowed to move in flight.

D. There is no suitable food for them in flight.

2. Generally, which of the following pregnant woman should issue the diagnosis proof? _____

A. The woman whose pregnancy is 27 weeks.

B. The woman whose pregnancy is 38 weeks.

C. The woman whose pregnancy is 33 weeks.

D. The woman whose pregnancy is 36 weeks.

3. What kind of items should a medical diagnostic certificate contain? _____

A. Name and age of passenger and their date of pregnancy.

B. Flights and dates of travel.

C. Whether or not they are fit for air travel or have any special requirements.

D. All the above.

4. The medical diagnostic certificate should be issued within _____ hours prior to the departure.

A. 72          B. 24          C. 48          D. 36

5. Which of the pregnant woman will not be accepted for transportation? _____

A. The woman whose pregnancy is 27 weeks.

B. The woman whose pregnancy is 35 weeks.

C. The woman whose pregnancy is 33 weeks.

D. The woman whose pregnancy is 37 weeks.

## Words and Expressions

oxygen [ˈɒksɪdʒən] *n.* 氧气

pregnant [ˈpregnənt] *adj.* 怀孕的

restrict [rɪˈstrɪkt] *v.* 限制

exceed [ɪkˈsiːd] *v.* 超过，超出

diagnosis proof 诊断证明

aforementioned [əˈfɔːmenʃənd] *adj.* 上述的

issue [ˈɪʃuː] *v.* (正式) 发给

Culture Notes

## 无成人陪伴儿童乘机服务

假期到了,又到了无成人陪伴儿童的出行高峰期。很多情况下,父母因为工作或其他原因不能亲自陪同需要出国留学/度假/探亲访友的未成年子女一起乘机前往目的地。而针对这一情况,许多航空公司推出了"无成人陪伴儿童乘机服务"。那么这种服务是否安全?如何申请?

一、哪些儿童可以申请无成人陪伴服务?

无成人陪伴旅客是指年龄满5周岁但不满12周岁(有些航空公司会对年龄更宽泛)、乘坐飞机时无成人(年满18周岁且有民事行为能力的人)陪伴同行的儿童,简称UM。航空公司对此类乘客提供的服务,叫作"无成人陪伴儿童乘机服务",也就是我们常说的"儿童托运"。

无成人陪伴儿童服务仅限直达航班。每架航班可为无成人陪伴儿童提供服务的数量是有一定限制的,如果购票时家长未提出办理无陪儿童服务的申请,并且当天需要乘坐的航班无陪旅客人数已达到上限,航空公司将不会接受无陪旅客的申请。具体情况,要以各航空公司通知为准。

二、无成人陪伴服务申请方法

国内航班最晚在飞机起飞前一天的15点之前申请,国际航班在飞机起飞前48小时申请。由儿童的监护人或监护人的授权委托人前往航空公司的直属售票处或拨打热线电话等方式提出无成人陪伴儿童乘机申请,并按要求办理相关手续。

通过申请后,乘机当天需在起飞前120分钟到达航班始发地机场办理乘机登记手续,送站人需要携带《无成人陪伴儿童乘机申请书》(一式两份)。为无成人陪伴儿童办完乘机手续后,其送站人应停留在机场,直至航班起飞。到达目的地后,服务人员按《无成人陪伴儿童乘机申请书》内容查验儿童接机人证件,交接无成人陪伴儿童,请接机人员在《无成人陪伴儿童乘机申请书》上签名。

## Text B

## The Rules about Pets in Air China

Small animals are defined as domesticated dogs and cats. Animals prone to attack or injure humans like Tibetan Mastiff and Bulldog do not fall into the category of small animals.

Small animals must be accompanied by valid health and vaccination certificates and must be in compliance with the related regulations of the countries of entry, transit and exit in order to be accepted for carriage.

Small animals cannot be taken into the cabin but can be carried as checked baggage in the cargo compartment of the aircraft.

Small animals are classified as special baggage and are subject to special baggage charges.

The total weight of one container for the small animal(s), including the feed and water shall not exceed 32kg. Otherwise, the container shall be carried as cargo.

Up to two containers for small animals are allowed on each flight.

Small animals can only be accepted for carriage on Air China-operated one-way nonstop flights, but not on connecting flights for the time being.

Air China shall not be liable for any delay, such as, due of the animal, which is refused to entry into or transit through any country, state or territory; or for any injury, sickness, escape or death of the animal under normal conditions of carriage.

Request for the carriage of small animals shall be made at least 24 hours before flight departure at our designated ticketing offices. Since only some selected aircraft types are fit for the carriage of small animals, your animal can only be accepted for a carriage after we have given our consent and made proper arrangements in that regard.

You must check in your small animal at the airport no later than 120 minutes before flight departure. In that process, you need to provide all the documents required for the carriage of your small animal.

## Decide whether the statements are true or false according to the passage.

1. Bulldogs can be carried into the aircraft. ( )
2. The pets which are accepted for carriage should be charged as the special baggage. ( )
3. Pets can be carried only on the one-way nonstop flights. ( )
4. Air China should be responsible for the injury and sickness of the pets under normal conditions of carriage. ( )
5. Passengers traveling with pets should check in the small animals at least two hours before the flight takes off. ( )

## Words and Expressions

domesticated [dəˈmestɪkeɪtɪd] *adj.* 家养的
category [ˈkætəɡəri] *n.* 种类，范畴
accompany [əˈkʌmpəni] *v.* 陪伴，陪同
vaccination certificate 检疫证明
in compliance with 按照，遵照
carriage [ˈkærɪdʒ] *n.* 运输
compartment [kəmˈpɑːtmənt] *n.*（飞机、轮船或火车上的）车厢，舱
liable [ˈlaɪəb(ə)l] *adj.*（在法律上）有责任的
designated [ˈdezɪɡneɪtɪd] *adj.* 指定的
consent [kənˈsent] *n.* 许可，允许

## 残障旅客特殊服务

残障旅客除特殊情况外不应被拒绝乘机。残障旅客需要特殊服务时，要事先向航空公司提出申请，航空公司可以提供上飞机、下飞机及衔接航班的协助服务，包括人员和装备。航空公司应接受轮椅作为托运行李，但禁止旅客自行携带氧气。

### 出行建议

盲人或者持有医生证明的失聪旅客经航空公司同意可以携带导盲犬或助听犬乘机。导盲犬或助听犬连同其容器和食物，可免费运输且不计算在免费行李额内。带进客舱的导盲犬或助听犬，必须在上飞机前戴上口套和牵引绳索，并不得占用座位，也不得让其任意跑动。货舱运输的导盲犬或助听犬还要符合关于小动物的相关条件。

### 护理

可确定其空中旅行是否需要乘务员特殊照顾，出现下列情况之一者，航空公司有权决定乘务员是否需要给予安全上的协助。

① 由于精神不健全而不能理解或遵循安全指导；
② 由于身体不健全、残疾而自身不能进行紧急撤离；
③ 由于听力或视力不健全而不能接受必要的指导；
④ 需要他人协助进行医护治疗，包括注射。

### 乘机要求

① 航空公司为了安全、技术上的原因，可以限制在其任何航班上接受各类残障旅客的数量，737机型执飞的航班，每一航段最多承运1名担架旅客或轮椅旅客，CRJ机型每一航段最多承运1名轮椅旅客，不承运担架旅客；
② 不得安排残障旅客坐于应急出口或靠通道的座位，也不得安排其直接与另一位类似的旅客同排就座，737机型承运担架旅客时如需拆除座椅，由机务负责在旅客登机前将客舱最后三排右侧座椅拆除；
③ 紧急情况下，指定两名援助者协助残障旅客撤离飞机。

## Part Four   Speaking for Communication

**Directions:** Act out the conversations with your partners.

### Conversation A   Infant Service

Conversation A

（FA=Flight Attendant, P=Passenger）

Scene: A flight attendant finds that a baby can't stop crying when coming around in the cabin. She comes up to the lady to offer some help.

FA: Madam, the baby is crying. Would you like some help?

P: Yes, Miss. I'm sorry about the noise. I think he must be hungry.

FA: Have you taken powdered milk with you? Can I help you with the powdered milk?

P: Yes. The baby's bottle and powdered milk are in the overhead compartment. Would you please get them for me?

FA: Of course, I will get them for you.

P: Could you get me some warm water and mix the powdered milk with it, please?

FA: No problem.

P: Please use the spoon to take three teaspoons of milk powder, then add 60ml water into the feeding bottle and shake a while.

FA: OK.

(A minute later)

FA: Here is the milk. I also bring you a toy, and I hope he'll like it.

P: Thank you. You are so considerate.

FA: Is there anything else I can do for you?

P: I also need to change the baby diaper. And I'd like to know where I can do it.

FA: You can use the changing board in the lavatory. If you need any help, please don't hesitate to call me at any time.

P: Thank you so much.

FA: You are welcome, Madam.

## Words and Expressions

powdered milk 奶粉
overhead compartment 行李架
teaspoon ['tiːspuːn] *n.* 一茶匙的量
diaper ['daɪpə(r)] *n.* 尿布，纸尿片
hesitate ['hezɪteɪt] *v.* 犹豫

## Conversation B　Senior Passenger Service

(FA=Flight Attendant, P=Passenger)

Scene: During the reception, the flight attendant had a conversation with the 70-year-old lady.

FA: Good morning, Ma'am. May I have your boarding pass, please?

P: Of course, here you are.

Conversation B

FA: Ma'am, your seat is in the 12B. I'll show you, and let me help you with your baggage.

P: Thank you very much, girl.

FA: This is your seat. Please have a seat. Would you like to put your baggage on the overhead compartment or under your seat?

P: It's OK to put it under the seat.

FA: OK, let me help you.

(After a while)

FA: Ma'am, this is the blanket for you. I'd like to cover it for you. You may push the button on the armrest to lean back your seat, so that you will feel more comfortable. The ventilator is above your head, and if you feel cold, you can turn it to the right to shut off. Lavatories are located in the front of the cabin and in the rear. If you need any help, press the call button to let me know.

(Two hours later)

FA: Hello, Ma'am, the plane is about to land. It is very cold outside. Please dress warmly before going out. Do you have a coat in your carry-on baggage?

P: Yes, there is one in my bag. You can find it easily after opening the bag.

FA: Let me help you with it.

P: Thank you, girl.

FA: You're welcome.

## Words and Expressions

blanket [ˈblæŋkɪt] *n.* 毯子

ventilator [ˈventɪleɪtə(r)] *n.* 通风设备

# Part Five　Case Study

案例一：2019年4月21日，在一架从吉隆坡飞往澳大利亚珀斯的飞机上，一位怀抱婴儿的妇女突然从座位上站起来，面色惊慌地哭喊："有医生吗？"原来，这位妇女的两个月大的婴儿在飞机起飞10分钟后，突然面色苍白、呼吸骤停。两位医生前来施救，飞机紧急降落，孩子被送往医院，但遗憾的是，孩子还是因为病情过重，没能抢救过来。请问，多大的婴儿可以乘坐飞机？

案例二：7月6日，MU2239南昌到西安航班上迎来了一位"无成人陪伴儿童"，乘务员和小旅客交流着，努力让她尽快适应陌生的环境，打消紧张的情绪。请分析一下针对无成人陪伴儿童的个性化服务包含哪些内容。

# Part Six  Further Practice

## Task 1  Writing

**Directions:** Write an announcement for providing service to special passengers by using the following words or expressions:

pursers, flight attendants/crew members, working experiences, take care of/provide service for, special passengers

Announcement

_____
_____
_____
_____

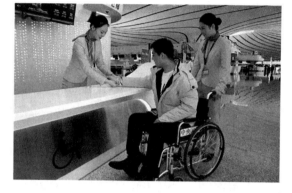

## Task 2  Translating

**Directions:** Translate the following sentences into English.

1. 你可以去洗手间给宝宝换尿布。

2. 呼叫铃在您头顶上方,需要任何帮助可以随时叫我。

3. 客舱的前部和后部都有洗手间。

4. 我来帮您拿行李。

5. 女士,这是给您的毛毯。

6. 您可能需要更换机上专用轮椅。

7. 需要我帮你把小背包放进行李架吗?

8. 对不起,导盲犬不能占座。

## Task 3  Story Reading and Retelling

**Directions:** Read the following story in a group and retell it to your group members in your own words.

A passenger told air hostess that he needed a cup of water to take his medicine when the plane just took off. She told him that she would bring him the water in ten minutes.

The air hostess was so busy that she forgot to give him the water. As a result, the passenger was held up taking his medicine. Thirty minutes later, when the passenger's ring for service sounded, she hurried over to him with a cup of water, but he refused.

In the following hours on the plane, each time the air hostess passed by the passenger, she would ask him with a smile whether he needed help or not. But the passenger never answered a word.

When he was going to get off the plane, the passenger asked the air hostess to hand him the passengers' booklet. She was very sad. She knew that he would write down sharp words, but with a smile handed it to him.

Off the plane, she opened the booklet, and smiled, for the passenger put it, "On the flight, you asked me whether I needed help or not for twelve times in all. How can I refuse twelve sincere smiles?"

That's right! Who can refuse twelve sincere smiles from a person?

## Task 4  Situational Conversation

**Directions:** The subject matters are given below for several kinds of conversations between the flight attendants and the passengers. Make up short dialogues—four or five lines—that could develop from these situations. Act out the conversation with your partners.

1. During the beverage service, the flight attendant provides a pregnant passenger with proper beverage.

2. Mary wants to change the diaper for her baby, but unfortunately she finds that she forgot to bring the diapers. The flight attendant comes to ask if she needs any help.

3. Mr. Li is traveling with his four-year-old son and it is the first time for his son to take the plane. So he would like his boy to take the window seat and asks for exchanging seats.

4. A 70-year-old passenger feels a little cold in cabin. The flight attendant comes to provide some help.

5. A blind passenger wants to go to the lavatory, and the flight attendant comes to provide some help.

| | Commonly Used English for Special Passengers |
|---|---|
| Pregnant passengers | There are lavatories in the front and rear of the cabin. |
| | Let me help you put the pillow around your waist, so that you will feel more comfortable. |
| | Do you have a permit to fly by the doctor? |
| | Iced beverage is not good for a pregnant woman. |
| | Please let us know if you feel uncomfortable. |
| | Please don't hesitate to ask me for help whenever you need it. |
| Passengers with infants | Would you like me to take a baby seat belt for you? |
| | If you want to change the baby diaper, you can go to the lavatory. |

| Commonly Used English for Special Passengers ||
| --- | --- |
| Passengers with infants | We have baby bassinets on board. |
| | This seat is for infants especially. |
| | This is the baby meal you ordered. |
| | We offer fresh milk to infants. |
| | Please be sure not to leave him alone. |
| Unaccompanied minors | May I help you put your small bag into the overhead compartment? |
| | Here are some comic books. |
| | I can tell you a story/joke. |
| | Open the door of the lavatory like this. Be careful, don't hurt your fingers. |
| | This is the child meal for you. Be careful, it's a little hot. |
| Disabled passengers | Our attendants will help you if you would like to go to the lavatory. |
| | You have to change the special wheelchair on board. |
| | We are entering the cabin now. Please hang on to your chair. |
| | May I introduce the meal for you? |
| | I'm afraid the guide dog can't take a passenger seat. |
| Senior passengers | Let me help you with your baggage. |
| | May I put your crutches under your seat? |
| | Do you need a pair of reading glasses? |
| | This is the blanket for you. |
| | It's very cold outside. Please dress warmly before going out. |

# Unit Three   Emergency Procedures
（应急救援）

After learning, you will be able to:

1. Master the key language points and useful expressions about Emergency Procedures;

2. Understand the responsibilities of attendants during the flight;

3. Work in teams to find out solutions to problems you might meet in flight;

4. Conduct a series of writing, reading, speaking and translating activities related to the theme of the Unit.

## Part One   Lead-in: Imperturbation

**Directions:** Imperturbation is one of the important qualities that we should have to possess, which can help us to conquer any difficulties. The following real story can explain this quality clearly. After reading it, please discuss with your partner about your understanding of the valuable quality—imperturbation.

Sichuan Airlines Flight 3U8633 prepared to land in Chengdu with a damaged cockpit windshield on May 14, 2018. The pilots of a Chinese passenger jet made an emergency landing after a cockpit windscreen was ripped out in mid-air. Two crew members on the Sichuan

Airlines flight were injured when the plane's window blew out as it cruised at 32,000ft with 119 passengers on board. The jet's flight control unit was badly damaged by the resulting sudden decompression. Some parts of the system were reportedly sucked out of the gaping window, which forced the pilots to fly manually before landing the airliner safely at the south-west Chinese city of Chengdu.

## Part Two  Listening as Comprehension

**Directions**: Listen to the following two announcements and fill in the blanks according to what you hear, then create an announcement based on the substitutions given and speak it out.

### Announcement A

### Emergency Landing/Ditching

Ladies and Gentlemen,

Attention please! It is necessary to make an 1) _____ landing. The 2) _____ have been well trained to handle this situation. We will make every effort to ensure your safety, keep calm and pay close attention to the flight attendants and follow their 3) _____.

Announcement A

Please pass your food tray and all other service items for pick up.

Please put the high-heeled shoes, dentures, necklaces, ties, pens, earrings, watches and jewelry in the overhead bin or hand them to the flight attendants.

4) _____ your seat belt, bring your seat backs to the upright position and stow all tray tables. Stow footrests and in-seat video units. Please put all of your baggage under the seat in front of you or in the overhead 5) _____.

(Now the flight attendants will explain the use of life vest. Please put your life vest on and follow the instructions of your flight attendants.)

Now the flight attendants are pointing to the exits nearest to you. Please identify them and be aware your closest 6) _____ may be behind you. When 7) _____, leave everything on board!

Now we will explain to you brace position against impact. When instructed to brace against

impact, put your legs apart, place your feet flat on the floor. 8) _____ your arms like this, lean forward as far as possible, hold the seat back in front of you and rest your face on your arms.

(When instructed to brace against impact, cross your arms above your head, then bend over, keep your head down, and stay down.)

Thank you for your cooperation.

## Words and Expressions

high-heeled 高跟的
denture [ˈdentʃə(r)] n. 假牙
necklace [ˈnekləs] n. 项链
jewelry [ˈdʒuːəlri] n. 珠宝
life vest 救生衣
instruction [ɪnˈstrʌkʃn] n. 用法说明；指示

## Speaking A

Speaking A

**Directions:** Imitate the above announcement to make an announcement according to the following substitution.

### Substitution

1. Please put the { high-heeled shoes / necklaces / ties / earrings } in the overhead bin or hand them to the flight attendants.

2. Please put { your baggage / your hand bag } in the overhead compartment.

3. Now we will explain the use of { life vest. / oxygen mask. }

4. Fasten your seat belts immediately. The plane will make an emergency landing because of the { sudden breakdown of an engine. / heavy precipitation. }

## Announcement B

Announcement B

## Decompression

Ladies and gentlemen, our plane is now being depressurized. Oxygen masks have dropped from the compartment above your seats. Fasten your seat 1) _____; pull a 2) _____ sharply toward you and place the mask over your

nose and mouth. Pull the elastic 3) _____ over your head. Remain 4) _____ and breathe normally. If you are traveling with a child, attend to yourself first and then to the child. 5) ____ is not allowed.

## Words and Expressions

decompression [ˌdiːkəmˈpreʃn] *n.* 客舱失压
drop [drɒp] *v.* 投，丢
breathe [briːð] *v.* 呼吸
elastic [ɪˈlæstɪk] *adj.* 有弹性的

## Speaking B

**Directions:** Imitate the above announcement to make an announcement according to the following substitution.

Substitution

Speaking B

1. We will begin the preparation for { our ditching. / emergency landing. }

2. Please remain calm and follow the { directions / instructions } from your flight attendants.

3. The flight has been delayed due to { some mechanical troubles. / ground fog. }

4. Thank you for your { cooperation. / assistance. / understanding. }

# Part Three   Reading as Acquisition

## Text A

## Emergency Procedures

As long as there have been aircrafts, there have been unexpected events that have emergency procedures in order to help ensure the safest possible outcome for both aircraft and people. In aviation, emergencies are defined as situations in which immediate action by those involved is required in order to ensure the safety of a flight. In general, humans are well equipped to deal consistently and effectively with emergencies.

A detailed set of guidelines or procedures for people to follow in the event of an emergency often helps to positively impact the emergency situation. These procedures have evolved from the relatively simple memorized procedures used by pilots of early aircraft to the relatively complex procedures used by flight crew.

Emergency procedures range from small-aircraft checklists for dealing the accidental opening of a cabin door during flight to large commercial airports' detailed emergency plans for dealing with an incoming aircraft that has been rendered virtually uncontrollable.

### Procedures in the Aircraft

In a small aircraft, it is recommended that pilots carry a set of emergency procedure checklists readily available to them in the event of an emergency. These checklists may be in paper or electronic format. Emergency procedures cover a variety of topics dealing with engine failures, in-flight fires, electrical failures, flight control malfunctions and others.

Generally, the more the aircraft is complex, the more emergency procedures are involed. In larger transport aircraft, more than one pilot is available to assist during crisis situations, and the delegation of responsibility at such times rests upon the pilot in command. In an emergency situation involving a multi-crew aircraft, generally one pilot continues to fly and maintain control of the aircraft while the other pilot (or two) is freed up to focus on the emergency procedures.

### Electronic Aids

In modern aircraft with electronic flight instrumentation there are often systems onboard the aircraft that will assist the flight crew in diagnosing a problem and provide the appropriate checklist on what is called a multifunction display (MFD) on the flight deck. This display highlights the appropriate checklist items and forces the crew to acknowledge each checklist item before proceeding to the next item.

Larger aircrafts, such as the Boeing 757 and 767, are equipped with an engine information and crew alerting system (EICAS), which immediately brings a fault diagnosis to the attention of the flight crew.

### Cabin Safety

Emergency procedures also exist for the cabin crew, flight attendants, and passengers. All passengers are required by the Federal Aviation Regulations (FARs) to be briefed on these procedures by the cabin crew prior to flight. Research has shown that passengers who listen to the preflight emergency briefing information are much more likely to survive an air accident than those who do not.

Airline cabin crew members are required to attend annual recurrent emergency procedures training. This training consists of a review of basic emergency and evacuation procedures of the particular aircraft the crew members fly.

### Survival

In order to survive an air accident, the crew and passengers must be able to do three things successfully. First, they must survive the impact of the crash, if applicable. Second, they must evacuate the aircraft safely in a timely manner, especially in the event of a fire. Third, if the accident occurs away from an airport, they must survive the post-accident environmental conditions until they are rescued or until safety is reached. The first two things are often largely dependent upon how much attention was paid to the preflight safety briefing, whereas the third thing depends upon previous training.

## Please answer the following questions according to the passage.

1. What do emergency procedures cover in the case of small aircraft?
2. How do pilots assist during crisis situations in larger transport aircraft?
3. How is each crew member aware of the checklist item and its completion status?
4. Who are much more likely to survive an air accident according to the research?

## Words and Expressions

aircraft [ˈeəkrɑːft] *n.* 飞机，航空器
aviation [ˌeɪviˈeɪʃn] *n.* 航空，航空工业
consistently [kənˈsɪstəntli] *adv.* 一贯地，始终
guideline [ˈɡaɪdlaɪn] *n.* 指导方针，准则

pilot [ˈpaɪlət] n. 飞行员，领航员
checklist [ˈtʃeklɪst] n. 清单，检查表
accidental [ˌæksɪˈdentl] adj. 意外的，偶然的
render [ˈrendə(r)] v. 使成为，使处于某种状态；给予
malfunction [ˌmælˈfʌŋkʃn] n. 故障，失灵
delegation [ˌdelɪˈgeɪʃn] n. 代表团
rest upon 依赖于，取决于
command [kəˈmænd] n. 命令，指示
diagnose [ˌdaɪəgˈnəʊz] v. 诊断（病症）；找出原因
proceed [prəˈsiːd] v. 开始行动，开展
briefing [ˈbriːfɪŋ] n. 情况介绍会；简报
evacuation [ɪˌvækjuˈeɪʃn] n. 撤离，疏散
applicable [əˈplɪkəb(ə)l] adj. 适用的，适当的

## 迫降

　　迫降（forced landing）指飞机因意外情况不能继续飞行而在机场或机场以外的地面或水面上进行的有意识紧急降落。因迫降对落点环境及飞行器的性能要求很高，所以存在着较大风险，常有可能机毁人亡。导致迫降的意外情况有：飞机的机械、液压或电气设备失灵（如起落架无法展开），发生火灾，在空中与别的飞机或物体相撞，机上人员伤病、有生命危险，飞机迷航燃料用尽，天气条件突然变坏，出现劫机或非法越境、不服从空中交通管制等情形。

　　迫降一般分为陆上迫降和水上迫降。陆上迫降指着陆场地在陆地，水上迫降指着陆场地在海洋、湖泊等水面上。水上迫降要求尽可能靠近陆地。水上迫降危险性高于陆上迫降。在机场内着陆时，若起落架不能自动放下，则用手控放下；如手动无效，则用机腹擦地着陆。

## Text B

## Heavy Precipitation

　　Thunderstorm and well-developed cumulus clouds produce heavy precipitation at all levels, in the form of hail or very heavy rain. When an airplane encounters huge hailstones, especially in tropical latitudes, damages may run up to millions of dollars. It may lead to aircraft being grounded for very expensive repairs that can include the need to re-skin part of the wing, fuselage or tail. In some parts of the world, thunderstorms are so frequent and widespread that airliners cannot avoid them. In these cases a careful pilot will slow the aircraft to a safe speed so as to minimize damage and will ensure that passengers and crew use seat belts and loose articles are stowed.

Very heavy rain is less dangerous to flight although there is evidence to suggest that the heaviest rainfall reduces aircraft performance. This has consequences for safety during take-off and landing but not normally during cruising flight. The risks of heavy rainfall are minimized by good design of runways and the use of porous (多孔的) runway surfaces. However, sometimes pilots have to delay take-off or landing until the excess water has drained from the runway surface. When flooding does occur on runways, tires can be damaged by water trapped between the tire and the runway turning to super-heated steam.

Heavy rain obscures pilot vision through the windshields. In the worst case, this can cause optical illusions from refraction that are particularly troublesome at night. To counter these effects, special liquids are sprayed onto windshields in the worst conditions of very heavy rain. The liquid used is difficult to handle and is not environmentally friendly. A later development is the use of a hydrophobic coating on windshields that is as effective. These coated windshields are standard on all newly-built Boeing airplanes.

## Decide whether the statements are true or false according to the passage.

1. Huge hailstones do little damage to the aircraft in flight. ( )
2. Very heavy rain is more dangerous to flight than a thunderstorm. ( )
3. The risks of heavy rainfall are minimized by good design of runways and the use of porous top surfaces. ( )
4. Heavy rain may cause pilots to experience an optical illusion. ( )
5. All newly-built Boeing airplanes are fitted with coated windshields. ( )

## Words and Expressions

precipitation [prɪˌsɪpɪˈteɪʃn] *n.* [化学] 沉淀物；降水；冰雹
cumulus [ˈkju:mjələs] *n.* 积云；堆积，堆积物
hail [heɪl] *n.* 冰雹
latitude [ˈlætɪtju:d] *n.* 纬度
fuselage [ˈfju:zəlɑ:ʒ] *n.* 机身（飞机）
drain [dreɪn] *v.* （使）排出，滤干
dual [ˈdju:əl] *adj.* 双的，双重的

modification [ˌmɒdɪfɪˈkeɪʃn] *n.* 修改
obscure [əbˈskjʊə(r)] *v.* 遮掩，遮蔽
refraction [rɪˈfrækʃn] *n.* 折射；折光
hydrophobic [ˌhaɪdrəˈfəʊbɪk] *adj.* 疏水的，不易被水沾湿的

## 恶劣天气对飞机的影响

### 1. 雷暴对飞行的影响

雷暴云是一个"天气制造厂"，它能生产各式各样的危及飞行安全的天气现象——强烈的湍流、积冰、闪电击（雷击）、雷雨、大风，有时还有冰雹、龙卷风、下冲气流和低空风切变。当飞机误入雷暴活动区内，轻者造成人机损伤，重者造成机毁人亡。因此，雷暴是目前被航空界、气象界所公认的严重威胁飞行安全的"敌人"。

### 2. 颠簸对飞行的影响

颠簸强烈时，飞行员操纵飞机困难，甚至暂时使飞机失去控制，或者使飞机结构遭到破坏，造成机毁人亡的事故。颠簸使机身震颤，会使进入发动机气道的空气量显著减少，严重时会造成自动停车。强的颠簸会使机组和旅客十分疲劳，头昏眼花，恶心呕吐。特别是突然强烈颠簸，如果未系好安全带，有可能会造成乘客伤亡。

### 3. 风切变对飞行的影响

风切变表现为气流运动速度和方向的突然变化。飞机在这种环境中飞行，相应地就要发生突然性的空速变化，空速变化引起了升力变化，升力的变化又引起了飞行高度的变化。如果遇到的是空速突然减小，而飞行员又未能立即采取措施，飞机就要掉高度，以至发生事故。

## Part Four   Speaking for Communication

**Directions:** Act out the conversations with your partners.

### Conversation A   Comforting a Passenger in a Severe Turbulence

Scene: The flight meets a severe turbulence. The plane is shaking terribly. Flight attendant Laura tries to comfort the passengers.

(P=Passenger)

P: Excuse me, Miss. Why is the plane shaking terribly? It makes me very uncomfortable.

Laura: I'm sorry to say that we hit some unexpected turbulence. Please remain your seatbelts fastened and don't move along the aisle.

P: I wonder whether the turbulence is severe. What should we do now? I'm a little scared.

Laura: Don't panic! Our captain has full competence to deal with it. All the crew members of this flight are well trained for this kind of situation. So please follow our instructions.

P: OK.

(Ten minutes later, the plane flies normally. Then there comes a cabin announcement.)

Laura: Ladies and gentlemen, although we met a severe turbulence just now, our experienced captain has dealt with the difficulties successfully. So you needn't worry about it now. Yet I am sorry to inform you that the flight will land at an alternate airport due to the unfavorable weather conditions over Shanghai Pudong International Airport. We do apologize for any inconvenience and appreciate your understanding.

P: Excuse me, Miss. Where will we land?

Laura: We will land at Hangzhou Xiaoshan International Airport ten minutes later. We will stay there until the weather conditions improve. Further information will be given soon.

P: What are the unfavorable weather conditions?

Laura: The visibility in Shanghai Pudong International Airport is lower than the standard required by CAAC, so our flight is not allowed to land.

P: Oh, I see. But I will attend a conference in Shanghai tomorrow. How can I go there?

Laura: If only we receive the instructions permitted to fly over Shanghai Pudong International Airport, we will take off as soon as possible. I believe it won't affect your conference.

P: That's OK.

Laura: I'm very sorry for that. I sincerely hope you can understand me.

P: Well, I see. Thank you.

## Words and Expressions

turbulence [ˈtɜːbjələns] *n.* 骚乱，动荡；（空气或水的）湍流，紊流
aisle [aɪl] *n.* 走廊，过道
visibility [ˌvɪzəˈbɪləti] *n.* 能见度
conference [ˈkɒnfərəns] *n.* 会议
take off 起飞

## Conversation B  Arranging for Evacuation

Scene: The plane will make an emergency ditching because of oil leakage from the aircraft. All the crew members on this flight are arranging for the passengers to evacuate. A passenger with a child pushes the call button.

Conversation B

(FA=Flight Attendant, P=Passenger)

FA: Excuse me, Madam. Is there anything I can do for you?

P: Sir, I'm too nervous and scared. I can't find life vests for my son. Would you like to help me?

FA: Don't be nervous. First you should be seated and remain your seatbelt fastened, I will take the life vest from the overhead compartment for you. Here you are.

P: Thanks a lot.

FA: You put on your life vest quickly. It's under your seat. I'll help your son to put it on.

P: OK. May I inflate the life vest now?

FA: No, Madam.

P: Why not? It may be too late to inflate it outside the cabin.

FA: There will be no room inside the cabin if all passengers inflate their life vests. What's more, some sharp objects may damage the life vest on the way out.

P: I see.

FA: When you hear the brace command, please bend over more, place your head between your knees and hold your ankles. Meanwhile, you should help your son to finish the action.

P: OK. Sorry, sir. Just now I was so nervous that I didn't see the use of an oxygen mask clearly. Could you show me how to use it again?

FA: Sure, look, please pull the oxygen mask over your nose and mouth and breathe normally. Are you clear?

P: Well.

(The plane has landed safely. All passengers are evacuating. A passenger is crying "help".)

P: Help... help me.

FA: What's up?

P: I can't release my seatbelt! Save me quickly.

FA: OK, let me help you. Please leave the cabin quickly.

P: Can you get my handbag from the overhead bin?

FA: Leave your bags behind...go...go...quickly.

P: Where is the exit? I can't see anything.

FA: In the front. Hold onto the person in front of you, and follow him to the exit. Please remove your high-heel shoes and glasses.

P: My glasses! I need glasses.

FA: Remove your glasses. It's dangerous when using the emergency escape chute.

P: OK. Too horrible!

## Words and Expressions

ditching [ˈdɪtʃɪŋ] *n.* 水上迫降

inflate [ɪnˈfleɪt] *v.* （使）充气，（使）膨胀

evacuate [ɪˈvækjueɪt] *v.* 疏散，撤离

release [rɪˈliːs] *v.* 释放，解开

chute [ʃuːt] *n.* 瀑布；斜槽；降落伞；陡坡道

# Part Five  Case Study

案例一：某航班，颠簸过程中，旅客烦躁地按呼唤铃，无论乘务员如何温言解释，但旅客就是对这种颠簸感觉到不满，甚至质疑飞行技术，要求乘务员给自己一个投诉渠道，乘务员无奈，只得提供给旅客95530投诉电话，但旅客在投诉时不但表示了对航班颠簸的不满，同时也不满乘务员的服务态度。

案例二：某航空公司的航班因为"机械故障"造成飞机的延误，导致133名旅客停滞在某机场9小时，焦急万分的旅客在漫长无望的等待中，没有得到航空公司对此事的任何解释，因此非常不满，集体拒绝乘机，要求得到航空公司的说法。据空乘人员方面的解释：当日该航空公司的航班，在飞机起飞前机械发生故障。航空公司出于对乘客的安全考虑，当即通知乘客航班推迟起飞，"为了旅客安全"这样做一点没错，但旅客不明白的是，检修人员为何不提早发现，非要等到飞机快起飞了才临时发现？

# Part Six  Further Practice

## Task 1  Writing

**Directions**: Write an announcement that goes after fire extinguished by using the following words or expressions:

put out, cruise, as scheduled, assistance, cooperation

Announcement

_____

_____

_____

_____

## Task 2  Translating

**Directions:** Translate the following sentences into English.

1. 由于飞机遇到强气流，请马上系上安全带。

_____

2. 弯下身把您的头放在两膝之间，然后抱住双膝。

_____

3. 请调直座椅靠背，固定好小桌板，收起脚踏板。

_____

4. 由于飞机遇到了强气流，所以洗手间暂时关闭。

_____

5. 别担心，请保持安静，我们的机长有能力和信心安全着陆。

_____

6. 我们的飞机可能在备用机场过夜。

_____

7. 由于飞机漏油需要紧急迫降。

8. 飞机完全停稳之前请您不要解开安全带。

## Task 3   Story Reading and Retelling

**Directions:** Read the following story in a group and retell it to your group members in your own words.

I am a new flight attendant, and I worry about the irregular things happen on board. But one day I met the emergency situation that the cabin was depressurized. One of the passengers was scared and asked me: "Is it quite frightening when cabin is depressurized?" I thought I should stay calm at that moment, and explained: "Well, it's almost impossible to hold your breath during cabin decompression, so don't worry. Cabin decompression is nowhere near as bad as the movies. The cabin decompression can be divided into slow decompression and rapid decompression. A slow decompression is slow loss of cabin pressure. It may be caused by metal fatigue, a bomb explosion or weapon firing which breaks the seal." Then, the passenger asked: "Which one is more dangerous?" I replied: "I think rapid decompression is more dangerous, it is usually caused by structural damage or air leakage, the cabin pressure will lose quickly, and the crew and passenger will suffer anoxia, low temperature and may even be pulled out off the aircraft. Slow decompression is usually caused by pressurization or air conditioning system malfunction, it's hard to be noticed by the crew, they may be unconscious before they react it." After my explanation, the passenger totally understood it. I'm glad that I can help others with what I have learned.

## Task 4   Situational Conversation

**Directions:** The subject matters are given below for several kinds of conversations between the flight attendants and the passengers. Make up short dialogues—four or five lines—that could develop from these situations. Act out the conversations with your partners.

1. Suppose you are a flight attendant. The flight meets a severe turbulence and shakes terribly. One of the passengers is very uncomfortable. You try your hard to comfort the passenger.

2. A passenger smokes in the lavatory and the flight attendant hears the alarm. The attendant tells him that the behavior is forbidden and illegal. The passenger apologizes and promises not do it anymore.

3. Suppose you are the chief purser of the flight, how should you persuade the passengers to be subject to your instructions before an emergency ditching?

4. How do you explain to the passengers when the plane has to land at an alternate airport due to the bad weather?

5. The airplane is now being depressurized. A senior lady feels panic. As the flight attendant, you go ahead to calm her. After discussion, the lady feels much better.

| | |
|---|---|
| Concern & reassurance | What seems to be bothering you? |
| | Would you like me to do something for you? |
| | Hello, lady/sir. What can I do for you? |
| | Just take it easy. It is under control. |
| | Our captain has full competence to deal with it. |
| Response to inquiries | Don't be nervous. |
| | Don't panic! |
| Emergency situation explanation | There is a strong air flow in or out. |
| | Our aircraft is experiencing some turbulence. |
| | Our plane is now being depressurized. |
| | A minor fire broke out in the rear cabin. |
| | We are now passing through the ... |
| Response to complaints | I'm very sorry for that. I sincerely hope you can understand me. |
| | I'm sorry to inform you that ... |
| Emergency order | Fasten your seat belts immediately. The plane will make an emergency landing because of the... |
| | Oxygen masks will drop down from the compartment above your head if there is any change in the pressure. |
| | Life vest is under your seat. |
| | Don't inflate the life vest in the cabin and as soon as you leave the aircraft, inflate it by pulling down the red tab. |
| | Bend your head between your knees! |
| | Bend down and grab your ankles. |
| | Get the extinguisher. |
| | Please locate the emergency exit nearest to you. |
| | Brace for impact according to my instruction. |
| | Open seat belts. Leave everything behind and come this way! |
| | Please leave the cabin quickly. |
| | Jump and slide down! |

# Unit Four  Duty-free Shopping

（免税购物）

Unit Four

Learning Objectives

After learning, you will be able to:

1. Master the key language points and useful expressions about Duty-free Sales;

2. Understand the responsibilities of attendants during the flight;

3. Work in teams to find out solutions to problems you might meet in flight;

4. Conduct a series of writing, reading, speaking and translating activities related to the theme of the Unit.

## Part One   Lead-in: Guidance

Duty-free shopping is available on most international flights. Prices of in-flight duty-free items are usually much lower than retail stores since they are not charged duty. So passengers may take advantage of the price saving and buy items for their own use or as gifts for members of their family or friends. That's why duty-free shopping is sometimes also called the "gift" shop in the sky. Duty-free goods/items range from cosmetics, jewelry, accessories, confectionery, liquor, children's toys, etc.

1. What are duty-free items?

2. What kinds of duty-free goods will you suggest if a passenger asks for your advice?

## Part Two  Listening as Comprehension

**Directions**: Listen to the following two announcements and fill in the blanks according to what you hear, then create an announcement based on the substitutions given and speak it out.

### Announcement A

### In-flight

Ladies and gentlemen,

Good afternoon! In order to further meet your traveling 1) _____, we will provide you many local products and international brands. You can 2) _____ your goods from the duty-free magazine in the seat pocket in front of you. Your cabin attendant is pleased to 3) _____ you. All 4) _____ are shown in US dollars. Please check 5) _____ your cabin attendant for prices in other currencies. Most currencies and US dollars, traveler's checks, the major credit cards are accepted for your 6) _____. Have a good trip!

Thank you.

### Words and Expressions

brand [brænd] *n.* 品牌，商标
attendant [əˈtendənt] *n.* 服务人员
currency [ˈkʌrənsɪ] *n.* 通货，货币
purchase [ˈpɜːtʃəs] *n.* 购买

### Speaking A

Speaking A

**Directions:** Imitate the above announcement to make an announcement according to the following substitution.

### Substitution

1. In order to further meet your traveling needs, we will

provide you {
  many local products.
  various famous liquor.
  well-known cosmetics.
  wines of good quality.
}

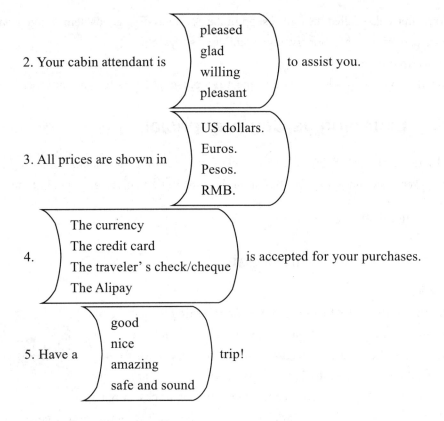

2. Your cabin attendant is { pleased / glad / willing / pleasant } to assist you.

3. All prices are shown in { US dollars. / Euros. / Pesos. / RMB. }

4. { The currency / The credit card / The traveler's check/cheque / The Alipay } is accepted for your purchases.

5. Have a { good / nice / amazing / safe and sound } trip!

## Announcement B

### In-flight Duty-free Sales

Ladies and gentlemen,

Announcement B

    We will begin our in-flight duty-free sales 1) _____ shortly. Our duty-free goods catalog(ue), with product information, can be 2) _____ in the seat pocket in front of you. For your convenience, we accept both 3) _____ and major international credit cards.

    For transit passengers, please note that liquid items purchased 4) _____ are subject to Safety Regulations on Prohibiting Liquid Items onboard. Please feel 5) _____ to contact any of our flight attendants for more 6) _____ .

Thank you very much!

### Words and Expressions

duty-free *adj.* 免税的 *adv.* 免税地
convenience [kənˈviːniəns] *n.* 方便，便利
transit [ˈtrænzɪt] *n.* 运输，运送 *v.* 经过，穿过
regulation [ˌregjuˈleɪʃn] *n.* 规章制度，规则
contact [ˈkɒntækt] *n.* 联系 *v.* 联系
liquid [ˈlɪkwɪd] *n.* 液体 *adj.* 液态的

## Speaking B

**Directions:** Imitate the above announcement to make an announcement according to the following substitution.

Speaking B

### Substitution

1. Is there a duty-free shop in the { departure lounge? / terminal building? / arrival lounge? }

2. He bought his { wife / aunt / uncle } a bottle of { perfume / red wine / rum } in the duty-free shop.

3. { 5% / 10% / 15% / 30% } off if you use this coupon at our duty-free shop.

4. The law permits you to bring in { two bottles of liquor / a carton of cigarettes / two boxes of perfume / a Rolex watch } duty-free if purchased in duty-free shops.

5. This { Sophisticated Blend / Chanel No. 5 / LV Montaigne / Ferragamo belt } is sold extensively in Asian duty-free markets.

## Part Three  Reading as Acquisition

### Text A

### World's Largest Duty-free Shop Opens in China's Sanya

The world's largest duty-free shop (DFS) opened its doors on Monday in coastal Sanya City in the southern island province of Hainan.

The Haitang Bay duty-free shopping center has attracted nearly 300 international brands. For several of them, including Prada, Rolex and Giorgio Armani, it is the first time they have appeared in a DFS on the Chinese mainland.

With a shopping area of 72,000 square meters, the center will replace an existing DFS, which is just one-seventh of the new store's size, in Sanya's downtown.

China International Travel Service Group (CITS) invested 5 billion yuan (about 814 million U.S. dollars) in the center, which is operated by China Duty Free Group under CITS.

The State Council, China's cabinet, gave Hainan permission to run a duty-free program on a trial basis in April 2011 to promote the island as a world-class international tourist destination by 2020.

From 2011 to 2013, Hainan saw an annual 15-percent increase in its tourism revenue on average, with offshore duty-free sales accounting for 10 percent of the total revenue.

Figures from the local customs show that as of mid-August, the revenue in Hainan's two duty-free stores exceeded 9.2 billion yuan.

## Decide whether the statements are true or false according to the passage.

1. The world's largest duty-free shop (DFS) opened its doors on Tuesday in coastal Sanya City in the southern island province of Hainan. (　　)

2. Those famous brands, including Prada, Rolex and Giorgio Armani, have appeared on Chinese mainland for the first time. (　　)

3. The Haitang Bay duty-free shopping center will replace an existing DFS, which is just one-seventh of the new store's size, in Sanya's downtown. (　　)

4. The government of Hainan gave Sanya permission to run a duty-free program. (　　)

5. From 2011 to 2013, Hainan saw an annual increase in its tourism revenue on average.
(　　)

## Words and Expressions

coastal [ˈkəʊst(ə)l] *adj.* 近海的，沿海的
mainland [meɪnlænd] *n.* 大陆
replace [rɪˈpleɪs] *v.* 取代，替换
invest [ɪnˈvest] *v.* 投资
operate [ˈɒpəreɪt] *v.* 操作，运行
cabinet [ˈkæbɪnət] *n.* 内阁
permission [pəˈmɪʃn] *n.* 同意，许可

destination [ˌdestɪˈneɪʃn] *n.* 目的地，终点；目标
revenue [ˈrevənjuː] *n.* 收入，收益；税收

## 免税和退税

免税就是买商品时免去税费，而退税是买完商品之后再将税退回。但是此税并非彼税。专家告诉我们，退税指的是退税购物 (tax-free shopping)，退的是增值税和消费税，税率集中在 5%~20%；而免税免的是进口关税(duty, tariff)，税率集中在 20%~100%。而你需要了解的是，当你看到 Duty-free 的字样，说明这是个免税店；而看到 Tax-free Shopping 的标志时，说明这家商店是可以购物退税的。

在可以退税的国家，大部分市中心百货商店、Shopping Mall、品牌店、购物村、工厂店等，甚至一些特色小店都可以退税。你可能会看到"Tax Refund"、"Tax-free Shopping"或"Euro Free Tax"等不同的退税标志，但只有在标有"Tax-free Shopping"标志的商店，你才可以选择回国退税。

## Text B

### American Airlines Discontinues Duty-free Sales on International Flights

American Airlines ended all in-flight sales of duty-free items late last week. The Fort Worth-based airline said that the move came following a dispute with its vendor.

"American Airlines has stopped selling duty-free merchandise on selected international flights as of Friday, March 20, 2015, due to a contractual disagreement between American Airlines and DFASS, the company that had handled our onboard duty-free sales", the airline told Frequent Business Traveler.

"The carrier is currently in the process of removing duty-free items, catalogs, and ads from its planes. Sales of duty-free items on some US Airways international flights 'will continue' until further notice", the airline said.

However, American is not the first major US airline to discontinue duty-free sales. Delta Air Lines ended in-flight sales last August following a dispute with the airline's duty-free vendor.

At the time Delta dropped its duty-free operations, a Delta purser, who asked that his name not be used as he was not authorized to speak on behalf of the airline, told Frequent Business Traveler he was "happy" to hear the news. He explained that he felt the change would improve the in-flight experience for passengers, who considered it more of a disruption than a benefit.

With the increase in duty-free stores at airports as well as the greater availability of goods

on the Internet, duty-free in-flight sales have been declining over the past decade.

While on-board sales have been discontinued, virtually all international airports offer duty-free shops where travelers can make purchases. Duty-free shopping can be traced back to the 1940s when Brendan O'Regan opened up a duty-free shop that sold Irish goods to passengers on a refueling stop at Rineanna (now Shannon) Airport where he served as catering controller.

## Questions for Discussion:

1. Why did the American Airlines stop selling duty-free goods?
2. Why was the Delta purser happy at the news that Delta dropped its duty-free operations?
3. What has happened to duty-free in-flight sales over the past decade? What's the reason for that?
4. When can duty-free shopping be traced back to?
5. How did the Delta purser feel about the change on duty-free operations?

## Words and Expressions

dispute [dɪsˈpjuːt] *n.* 争论，辩论  *v.* 对……提出质疑，否认；争论
vendor [ˈvendə(r)] *n.* 卖方，销售商
merchandise [ˈmɜːtʃəndaɪs] *n.* 商品，货品
contractual [kənˈtræktʃuəl] *adj.* 契约的，合同的
handle [ˈhændl] *v.* 拿；处理，应付
purser [ˈpɜːsə(r)] *n.* 乘务长，事务长
authorize [ˈɔːθəraɪz] *v.* 批准，许可
disruption [dɪsˈrʌpʃn] *n.* 扰乱
decline [dɪˈklaɪn] *v.* 下降，衰退
trace [treɪs] *v.* 发现，追踪

### 关于机上免税品

如今，全球各大航空公司的国际航班上都有机上免税品销售这一服务。通常是在国际航班起飞后一段时间到落地前，在机舱服务的过程中提供。在飞机上销售的货品卖点是"免税"，意味着价格更实惠。有时航空公司还会从品牌方获得一些独家在机

上销售的产品套装和优惠价,因此价格会更具吸引力。

据了解,航空公司国际航班上的机上免税品通常包括彩妆、保养品、香水、珠宝饰品、烟酒,以及航空公司的独家纪念品等。但是通常因为机上空间有限,这些免税品都是提前上机的,所以空乘人员的售货小车上不会有太多品种和单品,每一种产品一般只有一两件,卖完即止,因此会出现看中了买不到的情况。对此,航空公司近年来推出了网上预订的销售方式,比如乘客可在搭乘航班前的规定时间内,在航空公司的网站和机上免税品销售的专门微信或电话中订购,在机上可取到货。

## Part Four　Speaking for Communication

**Directions:** Act out the conversations with your partners.

### Conversation A　In-Flight Sales

Scene: A flight attendant named Della is serving the passengers, and a gentleman is choosing something beside the cart.

(P=Passenger)

Della: What can I do for you?

P: I want to buy something for myself.

Della: What would you like to buy?

P: I have no idea. Could you give me some advice?

Della: Certainly. We have a wide selection of fragrances, skin-care products, cosmetics, sunglasses, jewelry, watches, leather goods, cigars and some liquor, chocolate candies, children's toys, popular digital products and so on.

P: I'd like to buy some liquor. What kinds of liquor do you have, Miss?

Della: We have Glenfiddich, Chivas Regal, Johnnie Walker Red Label, Johnnie Walker Black Label, Rye Whisky, Dynasty, and Brandy. Which one would you like?

P: Both my father and I like to drink Whisky. Thus I decide to buy a bottle of Chivas Regal and a bottle of Johnnie Walker Black Label. One is for me, and the other is for my father.

Della: OK, wait a moment, please. Here you are.

P: How much should I pay you altogether?

Della: It comes to $ 58.00, Sir.

P: Can I have a discount?

Della: I'm sorry. All the items provided on board are at market prices.

P: May I use credit card?

Della: Sure, Sir.

P: Here is my card.

Della: Thank you. Please input your cipher.

P: OK.

Della: Please sign your name here.

P: Yeah. It is very nice of you to do all that for me.

Della: We are looking forward to serving you again someday.

## Words and Expressions

selection [sɪˈlekʃ(ə)n] *n.* 可供选择的东西

sunglasses [ˈsʌnglɑːsɪz] *n.* 太阳眼镜

cigar [sɪˈgɑː(r)] *n.* 雪茄烟

liquor [ˈlɪkə(r)] *n.* 烈性酒

Glenfiddich 格兰菲迪（纯麦威士忌）

rye [raɪ] *n.* 黑麦

Brandy [ˈbrændi] *n.* 白兰地酒

cipher [ˈsaɪfə(r)] *n.* 密码

## Conversation B  Duty-Free Items On Board

Scene: A flight attendant named Della is patrolling with a cart along the aisle, on top of which an attractive display of items is arranged. A woman is waving her hand.

(P=Passenger)

P: Excuse me, Miss. Do you sell duty-free items in the cabin?

Della: Yes, we will offer duty-free items in a while.

P: Do you have duty-free cosmetics on board?

Della: Certainly, here is the Duty-free Guide. Firstly, you may look it through. Then please tell me what you want.

P: OK. But would you give me some advice?

Della: Sure. We have perfume, lipstick, eye shadow/cream, face cream, skin milk and so on.

P: I want to buy a bottle of face cream. Which brand is better?

Della: I think Lancôme is OK. I like using it.

P: Is it expensive?

Della: It's 46 US dollars.

P: OK, would you like to get it for me?

Della: Certainly. By the way, would you like to buy something else?

P: Yeah, I nearly forget. My daughter asks me to buy a doll for her.

Della: I'm sorry, Madam. That has been sold out. This one is very popular today because tomorrow is Children's Day.

P: Could you recommend something for my daughter?

Della: How old is she?

P: She is twelve years old.

Della: How about all kinds of accessories?

P: Yeah, my daughter likes these things very much. Have you got anything brighter? Something more Chinese-style?

Della: Sure. What about the silk scarves? It's a conventional design and the colors are bright.

P: Yeah, very nice. Is it pure silk?

Della: Of course, pure silk.

P: This is very beautiful. How much is it?

Della: It's 25 US dollars.

P: Will I take it plus tax?

Della: All the items sold on board are duty free.

P: Would you accept traveler's check?

Della: Sorry, Madam. You need to pay in cash.

P: OK, how much are they together?

Della: Let me see. The face cream is 46 US dollars and the silk scarf is 25 US dollars. That comes to 71 US dollars.

P: It is 100 US dollars.

Della: Here's your change, 29 US dollars.

P: You've been most helpful.

Della: It's our duty to do this.

## Words and Expressions

cosmetics [kɒzˈmetɪks] *n.* 化妆品

perfume [ˈpɜːfjuːm] *n.* 香水；芳香

lipstick [ˈlɪpstɪk] *n.* 口红

eye shadow 眼影

accessory [əkˈsesəri] *n.* 装饰品，配饰

conventional [kənˈvenʃənl] *adj.* 依照惯例的，遵循习俗的；常规的

## Part Five   Case Study

案例一：某女士在某机场免税店购买了价值2800元的手提包，因涉嫌质量问题，与免税店进行交涉，期间有免税店客服表示"已销售商品不可以退换货"。你怎么处理这件事？

案例二：旅客在某月某日从洛杉矶——北京的航班上购买物品时，认为乘务员少找了10美元，双方意见不一致，乘务员打开自己衬衫上面的口袋，拿出10美元，几乎丢在旅客身上，并大声喊道：就算我赔你了！旅客对乘务员的态度和处理方法表示不能接受，强烈要求相关人员致歉和答复。如果你是该乘务员，会怎么做？

## Part Six   Further Practice

### Task 1   Writing

**Directions**: Write an announcement that goes before selling duty-free products by using the following words or expressions:

special service, toys, liquor, fragrances and cosmetics

Announcement

_____
_____
_____
_____

### Task 2   Translating

**Directions:** Translate the following sentences into English.

1. 为了满足您的旅行需求，我们将为您提供各种免税品。
_____

2. 如果您想了解其他货币标价，请咨询乘务员。
_____

3. 很抱歉，飞机上供应的商品都是明码标价的。
_____

4. 很抱歉我们不接受支票，你只能付现金或用信用卡。
_____

5. 先生您好，请问您想买点什么免税品？
_____

6. 这个化妆品太贵了，你能给我点折扣吗？
_____

7. 免税品宣传册就在您前面的座椅口袋里，您可以先浏览一下。
_____

8. 打扰一下，女士，请问飞机上卖免税品吗？

## Task 3  Story Reading and Retelling

**Directions:** Read the following story in a group and retell it to your group members in your own words.

In 2009, I began to work as a flight attendant. Earning my wings was my childhood dream that I had set for myself after my first plane ride at the age of five. Like so many others before me, I fell in love with the romance of airplanes and helping others.

I have flown hundreds of flights since graduation, but one stands out among them. We were flying from Los Angeles to Washington, D. C. when I found a young mother struggling with her baby. Everything was a mess, and the mother told me that she had no more diapers or other clothing on the aircraft. Through her tears, she informed me that they had missed their flight the previous night in Los Angeles. Since she hadn't expected to miss the flight, she was forced to use up most of her supplies and whatever money she had to support herself and her baby. As she stood in front of me, crying, I could see the hopelessness on her face. I immediately rang the flight attendant call button and asked for assistance from the other flight attendants. They brought cloth towels from the first class to assist in cleaning up both the mom and baby. I gave her a sweater and a pair of pants.

As she thanked me for all I had done, she said elegantly, "You're not the flight attendant, but you're a sky angel." Touching my flight attendant wings, she continued, "And those are your angel wings." Though I am no longer a flight attendant, my "angel wings" are still on display in my office. And each time I see them, I am reminded of that young woman, her son and the present that she gave me on that special day.

## Task 4  Situational Conversation

**Directions:** The subject matters are given below for several kinds of conversations between the customers and the salesgirl. Make up short dialogues—four or five lines—that could develop from these situations. Act out the conversation with your partners.

1. Suppose you are a salesgirl in the duty-free shop at the airport. You are talking to one gentleman who plans to buy a bottle of famous brand perfume. You give him some suggestions and help him buy the satisfactory perfume.

2. You are talking to a client about the discount of a leather handbag at the destination airport. She wants to know today's exchange rate and whether she can use the coupon. After explaining, she succeeds in buying a handbag with your help.

3. A lady intends to buy some qualified alcoholic drinks and tobacco for her father as Christmas gifts. She asks you which alcoholic drink and tobacco is good and suitable. You give her advice and help her choose the wine and tobacco.

4. A young passenger wants to know what in-flight duty-free items he can buy and whether he can pay by credit card.

5. A man wants to buy some duty-free cigarettes on board, but the attendant thinks he wants to buy 3 cartons of cigarettes which is not allowed on board. Explain to the passenger the relevant regulations on duty-free items.

| \multicolumn{2}{c}{Commonly Used English for Buying Duty-free Commodities} | |
|---|---|
| Concerns & inquiries | Good morning, Sir. Is there anything I can do for you? |
| | Would you like to buy some duty-free goods? |
| | Excuse me, may I have a look at the duty-free brochure? |
| | I wonder if I can pay by US dollars. |
| Responses to inquiries | Yes, I am interested in… |
| | You can pay by… |
| Inquiring needs and wants | Would you like some spirit or wine? |
| | What about your preference? |
| | Do you accept cash or traveler's cheque? |
| | Which brand of cigarette are you fond of? |
| Asking for regulations | How many cigarettes can I buy? |
| | Can I take more than 2 bottles of Remy Martin? |
| | What is the exchange rate today? |
| Explanations | You cannot buy more than 2 bottles of Vodka according to the regulations. |
| | You can pay for it in US dollars, UK pounds or Japanese yen. |
| Exchange rates | The exchange rate between US dollars and HK dollars is reasonable today. |
| | I think the exchange rate of Japanese yen against US dollar is good for the customer. |
| | US dollar against the RMB exchange rate has been declining. |
| Duty-free items | We provide high-quality duty-free items such as perfume, liquor, tobacco, leather ware, etc. |
| | You can buy qualified and famous products here without paying tax. |
| | Many passengers would like to buy liquor and tobacco in duty-free shops because in most countries liquor and tobacco have high taxes on them. |
| After-sale services | If you find any quality problem about our goods you can return the goods and get refunded. Please keep the receipt. |
| | We will supply you with 3-year global after-sale service once you buy this laptop. |
| | I'm terribly sorry for my mistake! Please give me a minute, and I'll bring a napkin to clean your clothes. |

# Unit Five   Landing

（着陆服务事宜）

Unit Five

**Learning Objectives**

After learning, you will be able to:

1. Master the key language points and useful expressions about safety check before landing and after landing, disembarkation of passengers and post-flight briefing;

2. Understand the responsi-bilities of flight attendants before and after landing;

3. Work in teams to find out solutions to problems you might meet before and after landing;

4. Conduct a series of writing, reading, speaking and translating activities related to the theme of the Unit.

## Part One   Lead-in: Smiling Service

**Directions:** Smile is an important skill that flight attendants should master in order to provide better cabin service. After reading a short passage about smiling service you may have a deeper understanding of the importance of wearing a smile to a flight attendant.

### Smile: A Key Way to Conduct Better Cabin Service

Smile is the universal language which conveys warmth, friendliness and kindness. It can help bring people closer to each other and can get us out of many tricky situations.

In the field of civil aviation service, smile is particularly important. It reflects a flight attendant's professional image, self-confidence and respect to others and helps to establish and maintain a good image and reputation of the airline.

Flight attendants have to deal with various passengers from all around the world. Sometimes the passengers can be annoying, picky and even rude. A smiling face can not only ease passengers' stress and fear, making them feel at home, but also play an important role when conflicts arise in the process of providing in-flight service.

Flight attendants are required by the airlines to keep smiling while serving passengers for the duration of the flight. They also receive training on the techniques to present the best smile in different situations. A qualified flight attendant should have the strong awareness to keep smiling when greeting and seeing off passengers, communicating with passengers and providing in-flight service for passengers.

Now discuss with your partner about your understanding of the importance of smiling service for a flight attendant and the ways to show the best manners to passengers during flight. Please take experience of yourself or others for examples to support your argument.

# Part Two  Listening as Comprehension

**Directions**: Listen to the following two announcements and fill in the blanks according to what you hear, then create an announcement based on the substitutions given and speak it out.

## Announcement A

### Safety Check and Thanks before Landing

Ladies and gentlemen,

May I have your attention please? Our airplane is expected to arrive in Beijing in approximately 15 minutes. We will be suspending our 1) _____. Lavatories have already been suspended. As we start our 2) _____, please make sure your seat backs and 3) _____ are in their full upright position. Make sure your 4) _____ are securely fastened and all carry-on luggage is stowed underneath the seat in front of you or in the 5) _____. For passengers sitting by the windows, would you please open the window shades? All personal electronic 6) _____ must be turned off, including your laptops and cell phones. We will be 7) _____ the cabin lights for landing.

On behalf of all crew members, we would like to thank you for your support and 8) _____ during the flight. We hope you enjoy your flight with us!

## Words and Expressions

suspend [sə'spend] *v.* 暂停
in upright position 处于直立状态
stow [stəʊ] *v.* 妥善放置，收好
window shade 遮光板
laptop ['læptɒp] *n.* 手提电脑

## Speaking A

**Directions:** Imitate the above announcement to make an announcement according to the following substitution.

### Substitution

1. We're scheduled to arrive in { Beijing / Tokyo / New York } in about { 10 minutes. / 15 minutes. }

2. There is a { twelve-hour / eight-hour / seven-hour } time difference between { Beijing / Shanghai }

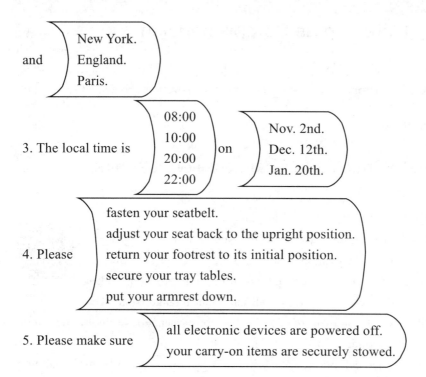

## Announcement B

### After Landing

Ladies and gentlemen,

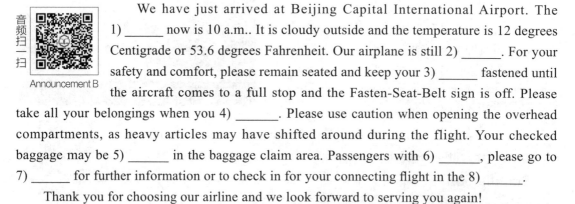

We have just arrived at Beijing Capital International Airport. The 1) _____ now is 10 a.m.. It is cloudy outside and the temperature is 12 degrees Centigrade or 53.6 degrees Fahrenheit. Our airplane is still 2) _____. For your safety and comfort, please remain seated and keep your 3) _____ fastened until the aircraft comes to a full stop and the Fasten-Seat-Belt sign is off. Please take all your belongings when you 4) _____. Please use caution when opening the overhead compartments, as heavy articles may have shifted around during the flight. Your checked baggage may be 5) _____ in the baggage claim area. Passengers with 6) _____, please go to 7) _____ for further information or to check in for your connecting flight in the 8) _____.

Thank you for choosing our airline and we look forward to serving you again!

### Words and Expressions

belongings [bɪˈlɒŋɪŋz] *n.* 所有物，行李
shift around 移动，变化
checked baggage 托运行李
baggage claim area 行李认领处
connecting flight 转乘航班

## Speaking B

**Directions:** Imitate the above announcement to make an announcement according to the following substitution.

Speaking B

### Substitution

1. Our plane has landed at { Shanghai Hongqiao International Airport. / London Heathrow International Airport. }

2. It is { sunny / cloudy / rainy } outside, with a temperature of { −15 / 20 } degrees Centigrade or { 5 / 68 } degrees Fahrenheit.

3. On behalf of { Air China / China Southern Airlines / China Eastern Airlines } and the entire crew, I'd like to thank you for joining us on this trip and we are looking forward to seeing you on board in the near future. Have a nice { day! / evening! / stay! }

4. As the outside temperature is relatively { high / low }, we suggest you { take off / put on } your coat when you disembark.

## Part Three  Reading as Acquisition

### Text A  The Cabin Crew Responsibilities During Landing

Takeoff and landing are the two most critical stages of flight. After getting notice from the flight crew, cabin crew will make preparations for the final descent for landing. They will make appropriate announcements regarding the expected time of arrival, the weather conditions and temperature at the destination airport, safety instructions and so on. A final cabin check must then

Unit Five  Landing（着陆服务事宜）

be completed prior to landing. Flight attendants must verify that all passengers fasten their seat belts, seat backs and tray tables are in the upright position, carry-on baggage is stowed, overhead compartments are closed and latched, passenger headrests and footrests are stowed, passenger earphones or headphones are removed, monitors are retracted, window blinds are open, etc.. They also need to make sure that aisles are clear, exits are not obstructed and the seating restrictions at emergency exit rows are adhered to. Besides, flight attendants also have to check that lavatories are vacated for landing and the lavatory doors will be locked. They will secure galley by stowing all service items safely, applying brakes on service carts, latching equipment, turning off electrical appliances, etc..

Once the cabin is secure and the cabin crew are seated at their assigned stations, the (chief) purser will confirm "cabin readiness" for landing to the flight crew. During landing, flight attendants will monitor the cabin and perform silent review of emergency procedures to get prepared for any emergencies that may occur.

After landing, flight attendant will remain seated until signal or announcement has been given by the flight crew. During taxiing, cabin crew will keep an eye on cabin conditions for any abnormalities and avoid passengers getting up to open overhead bins. When the aircraft stops completely, flight attendants will disarm the aircraft doors and check aircraft doors' status. After getting instructions, they will open the cabin doors. After-landing announcement will be conducted during this period, in which the cabin crew may give information regarding to the airport, connections, terminals and smoking lounges in the airport.

At the end of a flight, cabin crew members must remain stationed at exits and monitor the airplane and cabin as passengers disembark the plane. They also assist passengers with any special needs and small children off the airplane and escort children, while following the proper paperwork and ID process to escort them to the designated person picking them up. As soon as the last passengers leave the airplane, the cabin crew will perform cabin security check again and make sure that nobody forgot any luggage in the airplane, intentionally or not. If so, the items get handed off to ground staff.

### Decide whether the statements are true or false according to the passage.

1. Cabin security check is optional before landing since this has been done before takeoff. (     )

2. If the passenger has a lot of baggage, he could unfasten his seat belt and collect his belongings from the overhead bins during landing so that he could disembark earlier. (     )

3. When flight attendants are in their seat during landing, they should also monitor the cabin conditions from their seated positions since emergencies may occur in this critical stage. (     )

4. Passengers could unfasten their seat belts once the aircraft land on the runway. (     )

5. Flight attendants have to carry out security check after all passengers have left the airplane. (     )

## Words and Expressions

latch [lætʃ] v. 闭锁
retract [rɪˈtrækt] v. 缩回；缩进
window blind 遮光帘
obstructed [əbˈstrʌktɪd] adj. 阻塞的
vacate [vəˈkeɪt; veɪˈkeɪt] v. 空出，腾出
silent review 静默复习
disarm [dɪsˈɑːm] v. 解除（预位）
disembark [ˌdɪsɪmˈbɑːk] v. 下飞机
escort [ˈeskɔːt] v. 护送

### 驾驶舱与客舱的联系

飞行期间，正常情况下，飞行机组与客舱机组之间应通过内话系统进行联系，并使用普通话（当有外籍机组成员时，使用普通话和英语）。乘务员必须对驾驶舱附近保持警惕，使用标准联络信号进入驾驶舱。在夜间中远程飞行时，乘务员应至少每隔一小时进入驾驶舱一次，并进行适量谈话。

在飞行关键阶段［滑行、起飞、着陆和除巡航以外在3000米（10000英尺）以下的飞行阶段］，除非涉及飞行安全，乘务员应避免与驾驶舱联系。因乘务员不知飞行高度，通常可认为起飞后十分钟内和着陆前十分钟内已进入飞行关键阶段。

应急情况下，飞行机组可以通过旅客广播系统直接向客舱机组下达指令，使客舱乘务员能迅速准确地判断，准备处置的措施。

客舱机组与飞行机组之间联络使用的标准用语包括"急事，机长/Priority Captain""乘务长请到驾驶舱/Purser to cockpit please""客舱请完成下降准备/Cabin be ready for descent""机组各就各位/Crew at your station""原位坐好/Remain seated"等。

## Text B

## Post-flight Briefing

After each flight, cabin crew are required to attend a post-flight briefing hosted by the purser, which is also the final stage of their work. Usually post-flight briefings tend to be less formal and shorter in duration than pre-flight briefings.

A post-flight briefing is an important part of job for cabin crew. It typically involves the following:

### Discussion

The purser will make a briefing about the flight from the aspects of security and cabin service. Air security will also give an account of the safety work on board. A good post-flight briefing gives crew members the opportunity to discuss all onboard situations and issues, including service to special categories of passengers such as infants, unaccompanied children, persons with disabilities, inadmissible passengers and so on, resolving passengers' complaints due to missed drinks, wrong meals, turbulent conditions, minor ailments etc., emergencies and how they are handled during flight, passengers' advice and suggestions as well as other typical issues. It's important that any issues are discussed by crew to ensure that they have been resolved and to help prevent possible errors from re-occurring in the future.

### Feedback

During the post-flight briefing cabin crew will also receive feedback on their performance. Those with outstanding performance will be praised, while for the crew members who made mistakes, the purser may give advice on improvement or report to superior leaders if necessary. And the assessment results will be recorded in the cabin crew logbook. This can then be used by the cabin crew to improve their performance and help them progress.

### Money

Another part of a post-flight briefing is cabin crew counting the money they have taken in through sales of duty-free goods or other special products during flight. This is then used to assess how much money has been made on the flight, which cabin crew can use to work out how much commission they have made. This commission will contribute to the cabin crew's final salary.

### Documentation

It's also important to finalize all of the documents that are needed from the flight, for example, the flight report and summary of sales.

A post-flight briefing is the summary of the whole flight. It is beneficial for both the airline and cabin crew. Debriefing is important to identify things that went wrong or not as planned during the flight: any issues or emergencies, as well as planned and unplanned decisions. They allow any issues from the flight to be resolved and for the crew to receive feedback on their own performance. Therefore, it is possible for both the airline and crew to act on this feedback and make any adjustments to ensure that the airline provides better service to its passengers in the future.

## Please answer the following questions according to the passage.

1. What is the final stage of cabin service?
2. What are the differences between pre-flight briefing and post-flight briefing?
3. What will be discussed in post-flight briefing?

4. What will happen if a crew member has done something wrong during flight?
5. Why is it important to carry out post-flight briefing?

## Words and Expressions

post-flight briefing 航后讲评
air security 空中安全
give an account of 说明，叙述
category [ˈkætəgəri] n. 种类
infant [ˈɪnfənt] n. 婴儿
unaccompanied [ˌʌnəˈkʌmpənid] adj. 无人陪伴（或同行）的
inadmissible [ˌɪnədˈmɪsəbl] adj. 不许可的
ailment [ˈeɪlmənt] n. 小病
logbook [ˈlɒgbʊk] n. 日志
commission [kəˈmɪʃn] n. 佣金，回扣

## 针对不同乘客的客舱服务技巧

在乘务工作中，空乘人员在航班中会面对各种类型的乘客，也会遇到各种特殊事情。针对不同的乘客，尤其针对特殊乘客，乘务员应善于察言观色，能够迅速准确判断乘客的心理和服务需求，丰富自己的服务技能，为乘客提供更有针对性的服务。

初次乘坐飞机的旅客可能会缺乏必要的乘坐飞机的常识，因此会有紧张心理，空乘人员应避免轻视或嘲笑，要耐心讲解必要的乘飞机相关知识，并通过亲切的语言、肢体动作及表情等安抚他们的紧张情绪，使其安心。

对于外国旅客，乘务员应提前学习外语，以便在进行服务时流畅沟通，同时乘务员还应了解不同国家的风俗习惯，如宗教信仰、禁忌等，同样，对于不同民族的相关文化也应有所了解，这样就可以使用不同的服务方式、语言方式来服务乘客，使服务更到位、更贴心。

对于挑剔的乘客，空乘人员应避免急躁，不与乘客正面冲突，并以更大的耐心来倾听乘客的倾诉，用更加热情周到的服务使乘客平静下来，以使乘务员顺利开展各项工作。

对于有特殊需求的旅客，空乘人员应针对其特点提供有针对性的服务，例如带小孩的乘客在旅途中会有很多不便，如孩子的哭闹、喂食等，乘务员应给予特别关注，及时提供帮助。对于有疾病的乘客，乘务员应在飞行中密切关注，必要时给予救助。

对于重要乘客（VIP），由于其有一定的身份和地位，空乘人员在服务时要注意语言得体，注意礼貌礼节，服务要精心，关注细节，针对其心理需求提供相应的服务。

# Part Four  Speaking for Communication

**Directions:** Act out the conversations with your partners.

## Conversation A    Security Check before Landing

Conversation A

（CC=Cabin Crew, P=Passenger）

CC: Excuse me, Sir. Would you please take your seat and fasten your seat belt?

P1: I have a lot of items. I want to collect them from the overhead compartment earlier.

CC: Don't worry. There will be enough time for you to collect your belongings. And I will assist you with your bags.

P1: That's very kind of you.

CC: Excuse me, Madam. Would you mind returning your seat back to the upright position?

P2: I've no idea how to do it.

CC: Let me help you. Just press the button on your armrest. It's OK now.

P2: Thanks. By the way, can I use the lavatory now?

CC: The lavatory is still available for 5 minutes since the plane is making its final descent. Please be hurry.

P2: Thank you.

CC: Excuse me, Sir. Please switch off your cell phone as we are descending now.

P3: It's a very important call from my boss. I will finish it soon.

CC: I understand. But electronic devices may interfere with the normal operation of aircraft navigation and communication systems. For your safety, they must be turned off during takeoff and landing.

P3: All right.

CC: Thank you for your cooperation.

## Words and Expressions

item [ˈaɪtəm] *n.* 物品
descent [dɪˈsent] *n.* 下降
switch off 关闭
interfere [ˌɪntəˈfɪə(r)] *v.* 干扰
navigation system 导航系统

## Conversation B    Farewell

Conversation B

(FA=Flight Attendant, P=Passenger)

FA: Excuse me, Sir. The plane hasn't stopped completely. You can't leave your seat.

P1: OK. By the way, how is the weather at present?

FA: According to the latest weather report, it's raining outside and it won't stop until 2 p.m.. The temperature now is 7 degrees centigrade. It's a bit cold with strong northeast wind. You'd better take more clothes.

P1: Thank you very much.

FA: My pleasure.

(After a while)

FA: Ladies and gentlemen, our plane has stopped completely. Please don't be so hurry and get off in order.

FA: Ma'am, please watch your steps. It's slippery outside.

P2: Thank you.

FA: I hope you enjoy your stay in Beijing. We look forward to seeing you again.

P2: Thank you. Goodbye.

FA: Ladies and gentlemen, we have a pregnant passenger here. Would you be kind enough to let her get off first?

P3: That's fine.

FA: Thank you.

FA: Ladies and gentlemen, there is a passenger with limited mobility, would you please make a way for him and let him get off first?

P4: Okay.

FA: Watch your step, Sir. May I help you down the stairs?

P5: No, thanks. I can manage it. By the way, I am very satisfied with your service and I will choose your airline for my next flight.

FA: We hope to see you on board again soon. Goodbye.

P5: Bye.

## Words and Expressions

watch your steps 小心脚下
slippery [ˈslɪpəri] *adj.* 滑的
make way for sb. 给某人让路

# Part Five  Case Study

案例一：一位女士带着一个两岁多的孩子乘坐晚航班，在飞机下降过程中被乘务长唤醒，且熟睡的孩子也被叫坐起来并系好安全带。旅客问乘务长是否可以抱着孩子，乘务长回答"不可以"。旅客因为没有经验，故而再次询问，乘务长不但没有提供帮助，反而用质问的语气说："你觉得小朋友是坐着安全还是抱着安全？"请分析乘务员的做法并提供你的解决方案。

案例二：某航班上，一位旅客在刚播送飞机下降广播后想上洗手间，到后舱后，乘务员以飞机下降不安全为由阻止该旅客使用洗手间。在此期间，旅客发现该乘务员与其他机组成员聊天说笑，于是心生不满，并认为该乘务员工作不灵活，态度不认真，不能以身作则。请分析乘务员的做法并提供你的解决方案。

# Part Six  Further Practice

## Task 1  Writing

**Directions**: Write an announcement that goes before landing by using the following words or expressions:

seat belt, tray tables, switch off, carry-on items, pick up

Announcement

___

## Task 2  Translating

**Directions:** Translate the following sentences into English.

1. 我们的飞机很快就要着陆。为了您的安全，在机长关闭"系好安全带"指示灯之前，请在座位上坐好并系好安全带。

2. 感谢您乘坐我们的航班，希望有幸能与您再次见面。

3. 我们特别提醒您，请妥善保管您的小件物品，以免在降落期间滑落。

4. 我们即将关闭客舱灯光。如果您想阅读，我们建议您使用阅读灯。

_____

5. 需要转机的旅客请您到候机楼出发大厅办理登机手续。

_____

6. 对于本次航班的延误，我们深表歉意，并感谢您在航班延误时给予的理解与配合。

_____

7. 下机时请您带好您的全部手提行李。

_____

8. 您的托运行李请在到达厅行李领取处提取。

_____

## Task 3　Story Reading and Retelling

**Directions:** Read the following story in a group and retell it to your group members in your own words.

Before takeoff, a passenger asked a stewardess to bring him a glass of water to take the medicine. As the airplane was about to take off, the stewardess said to him politely: "Sir, the aircraft is expected to take off in 8 minutes. For your safety, please wait for a moment, and I will bring you the water as soon as the plane gets into a smooth flight."

20 minutes later, the cabin crew began serving food and drinks to the passengers. At this time, the stewardess heard a loud and rapid cabin service call and she realized that she forgot to bring the water to the passenger. Then she came to the cabin with a glass of water in a hurry. She said with a smile: "Sir, I'm terribly sorry. Due to my negligence, you didn't take your medicine on time." The passenger was very angry. He showed his watch to the stewardess and said: "Look, do you know how much time you have kept me waiting for the water? Is that the way you served the passengers?" No matter how she explained, the picky passenger refused to forgive her negligence. The stewardess felt frustrated but she still managed to keep wearing a smile and listened to the passenger's complaint with great patience.

During the rest of the flight, to make up her mistake, whenever the stewardess went to the cabin to serve the passengers, she would walk up to that passenger and asked with a smile if he needed water or other service. However, the passenger was still in anger and ignored the stewardess.

When the aircraft was about to arrive at the destination, the passenger asked the stewardess to bring him the comment book. Obviously, he wanted to make a complaint to the airline about the service of this stewardess. Despite the grievance, the stewardess brought the comment book to the passenger and again with smile on her face, she said politely: "Sir, please allow me to express my sincere apologies to you again. No matter what comments you are going to make, I will accept all your criticism." The passenger didn't say anything. He took the comment book and wrote on it.

After the last passenger left the airplane, the stewardess opened the comment book. To her surprise, the passenger wrote a letter of praise, in which he said he was deeply moved by the stewardess' sincere apologies, especially her smile, and due to the high-quality service, he would choose the same flight next time.

## Task 4　Situational Conversation

**Directions:** The subject matters are given below for several kinds of conversations between the flight attendants and the passengers. Make up short dialogues—four or five lines—that could develop from these situations. Act out the conversation with your partners.

1. Some passengers are complaining about the diversion of the aircraft. You apologize to them and explain the reasons. Besides, you try to comfort the passengers by offering some snacks and drinks. Finally, the passengers show their understanding and cooperation.

2. An elderly woman with mobility difficulties wants to fetch her belongings in the overhead compartment earlier. As the aircraft is about to land at the destination, you prevent her from doing so. And after landing you help her to disembark the plane.

3. An unaccompanied girl is on board. You assume the responsibility to take care of her. During flight, you will see to the child as long as you are free. As the aircraft is approaching the destination, the girl is worried whether she is able to meet her uncle successfully at the airport. Finally you make her relaxed and escort her to the designated ground handler successfully.

4. A passenger doesn't know how to adjust his seat back in upright position. You help him to solve the problem.

5. A foreign tourist flies to Beijing for his first time. He asks you about the time difference to set his watch and later you give him some travel guidance. He feels very satisfied with your service.

| | Commonly Used English for Landing |
|---|---|
| Giving orders and asking for permission | Would you please fasten your seat belt? |
| | May I trouble you to open the window shade? |
| | Would you mind stowing away your tray table? |
| | Please turn off your cell phone and electronic devices. |
| | I wonder if you could make way for the pregnant lady and let her disembark first. |
| Demonstrating the operation of sth. | Let me show you how it works. |
| | Just press the button under the armrest and lean back at the same time. |
| | You can do it like this. Put the table upright and then turn the knob. |
| Offering help | Is there anything I can do for you? |
| | May I help you with your luggage? |
| | Let me help you get off. |
| | Would you like me to help you? |
| | Need help? / Want a hand? |
| Expressing thanks | Thank you for your understanding and cooperation. |
| | I appreciate your support. |

| Commonly Used English for Landing ||
|---|---|
| Expressing thanks | Thanks a lot. |
| Reply to thanks | You are welcome. |
| | Don't mention it. It's our duty to do this. |
| | My pleasure. |
| Saying goodbye | See you again. |
| | Goodbye. Take care! |
| | We look forward to serving you again. |
| Warning and reminding | You shouldn't walk around in the cabin before the aircraft stops completely. It's dangerous! |
| | You'd better return to your seat. The aircraft is about to land. |
| | I'm sorry but you can't smoke for the duration of flight. |
| | Look out! /Be careful! |
| | Please watch your step. It's raining and rather slippery outside. |
| Lavatory | The lavatory has been suspended. |
| | I'm afraid you can't use the lavatory for now. The aircraft is about to descend. |
| Security check | Please make sure that your seat belt is securely fastened. |
| | As we have started our approach into the airport, the cabin crew will make a final check of the cabin to ensure that all baggage is stowed securely. |
| | Meanwhile, please note where the nearest emergency exit is located. |
| | As a safety precaution, it is important that you turn off all the electronic devices. |
| Disembarkation | Please wait until the air bridge is in its designated position. |
| | Now the plane has come to a complete stop. You can collect your belongings and prepare to disembark. |
| | Please get off from the front cabin door and go through the air bridge in order. |
| | Please take the shuttle bus when you get off the plane. It will take you to the arrival hall. |
| | The baggage claim area is in the arrival hall where you can see the signs guiding you there. |

# Unit Six  Customs Check
# （海关检查）

Unit Six

Learning Objectives

After learning, you will be able to:

1. Master the key language points and useful expressions about customs and immigration declaration, health quarantine, animal and plant quarantine;

2. Understand C.I.Q. laws and regulations and the responsibilities of attendants when carrying out international flight;

3. Work in teams to find out solutions to problems you might meet when instructing passengers to fill in C.I.Q. cards and the problems passengers might meet when going through Customs and Immigration;

4. Conduct a series of writing, reading, speaking and translating activities related to the theme of the Unit.

## Part One  Lead-in: Problem-solving Ability

**Directions:** Problem-solving ability is a crucial quality flight attendants should obtain to deal with any abnormal situations on board. After reading the following short passage you may have a deeper thought on the importance of developing such skill in order to make your work go well.

## Problem-solving Ability: A Must to Be a Good Flight Attendant

We can never predict what will happen when in the sky. Cabin crew need to be good at problem solving, since they may be thrown into new situations and encounter unexpected problems at any time. If this occurs during flight, they will need to figure out the best possible solution and try to resolve the situation to the best of their ability.

In emergencies, flight attendants rely on their training, knowledge and experience to navigate emergency situations and provide assistance to both passengers and the flight crew. What's more, problem-solving skills are also necessary for helping passengers resolve disputes and concerns compassionately and professionally.

Now discuss with your partner about your understanding of the importance of problem-solving skills for a flight attendant and how to develop such skills. Please take experience of yourself or others for examples to support your argument.

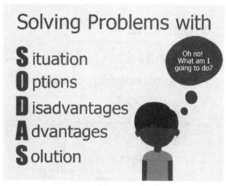

## Part Two  Listening as Comprehension

**Directions**: Listen to the following two announcements and fill in the blanks according to what you hear, then create an announcement based on the substitutions given and speak it out.

### Announcement A

### Filling out Entry Cards

Ladies and gentlemen, your attention please. Flight CA3205 is going to land at Shanghai Hongqiao International Airport in about 30 minutes. According to the 1) _____ of China,

...all arriving passengers are required to complete an 2) _____, a Customs Declaration Form and a Quarantine Form. You need to fill out these forms in Chinese or English and keep them with your 3) _____ together. Please provide your detailed 4) _____ in China and sign the forms in person.

Members of the same family should use one Customs Declaration Form. If you are not sure about the 5) _____ required for declaration, you can refer to the 6) _____ of the declaration form.

You are advised to complete these forms before reaching our destination in order to shorten the time through the customs and 7) _____ them to the officials from the Customs and Immigration on the ground.

If you need any assistance, please don't 8) _____ to call any of our cabin attendants. Thank you.

## Words and Expressions

customs declaration form 海关申报单
quarantine [ˈkwɒrəntiːn] n. 检疫
in person 亲自
refer to 参考
official [əˈfɪʃ(ə)l] n. 官员，高级职员
immigration [ˌɪmɪˈɡreɪʃn] n. 移民

## Speaking A

**Directions:** Imitate the above announcement to make an announcement according to the following substitution.

### Substitution

1. { Flight CA1590 / Flight MU5111 / The aircraft / Our plane } is going to land { at Beijing Capital Airport / at Heathrow Airport / in Shanghai } in about { 20 minutes. / 30 minutes. }

2. We will be distributing the { entry card / arrival card / Customs Declaration Form / Immigration Card / Health Declaration Form } in a few minutes.

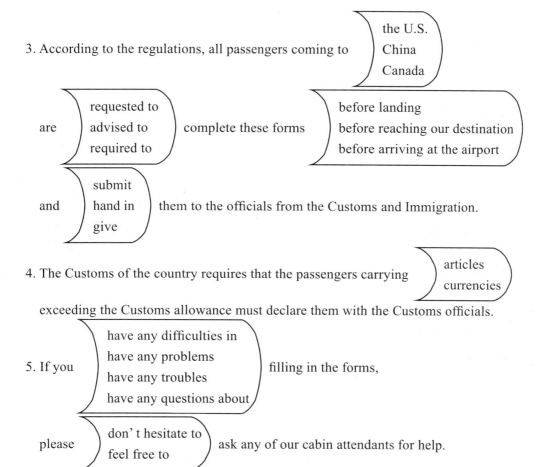

## Announcement B

## China Entry Quarantine

Ladies and gentlemen,

May I have your attention please?

In order to protect your health and the health of others, according to the "Frontier Health and Quarantine Law of the People's Republic of China", if you have any symptoms such as fever, cough, 1) _____, nausea, vomiting, diarrhea, 2) _____, muscle pains, joint pains, rash and so on, please 3) _____ our crews as soon as possible, or you might 4) _____ the quarantine officials later when arriving.

If you carry with or consign the following articles, such as microbes, human tissues, biological products, blood and blood products, please 5) _____ these items to China Inspection and Quarantine and go through the required 6) _____. Without permissions, you could not carry with or consign the items above.

Insects and animals, which might transmit 7) _____ are not allowed to carry, such as rodents, mosquitoes, cockroaches, etc.

You are welcome to follow this announcement. Any violations will incur the due 8) ____. For more information, please inquire the quarantine officials at the airport.

Thank you for your cooperation.

## Words and Expressions

Frontier Health and Quarantine Law of the People's Republic of China 中华人民共和国国境卫生检疫法

  symptom [ˈsɪmptəm] *n.* 症状
  diarrhea [ˌdaɪəˈrɪə] *n.* 腹泻
  rash [ræʃ] *n.* 皮疹
  consign [kənˈsaɪn] *v.* 托运
  rodent [ˈrəʊdnt] *n.* 啮齿目动物
  incur [ɪnˈkɜː(r)] *v.* 招致，带来

## Speaking B

**Directions:** Imitate the above announcement to make an announcement according to the following substitution.

Speaking B

### Substitution

1. According to the quarantine regulations of { the local government, / the U.S. government, / the Korean government, }

passengers are not allowed to bring in { fresh fruits. / cut flowers. / meat. / dairy products. / animal or plant products. }

2. Passengers who are in possession of such items must { dispose of them. / present them to the flight attendants. / make a declaration to the quarantine department. }

3. If you have symptoms such as { fever / dry cough / fatigue / breath difficulties } or any contact with patients with such symptoms in the past 14 days, or any travelling history in

{ Wuhan city / Tianjin city }, it is important for your own health and for the protection of others, that you { contact our crew members immediately. / bring this to the attention of any member of the crew. / consult the quarantine officials as soon as possible after landing. }

## Part Three  Reading as Acquisition

### Text A

## Customs, Immigration and Quarantine

Travellers, when departing or arriving in a country, need to fill out a Customs Declaration Form, an Immigration Declaration Form and a Quarantine Statement (C.I.Q.). Due to the different political and economic situations, customs, immigration and quarantine regulations may vary. Even for the same country, these laws and regulations also change with time. Despite these differences, C.I.Q. authorities or agencies perform similar basic functions.

Since international airports are the first point of entry to a new country, they have checkpoints in them through which travellers must pass before they leave the airport. Collectively, these are typically referred to as customs and immigration. Officials at customs and immigration are checking travellers for things like whether they have the right documents to be in the country, such as passport, visa, disembarkation card, etc., whether they're legally allowed to be there, and whether they're bringing anything illegal with them.

Specifically speaking, customs is responsible for collecting tariffs and for controlling the flow of goods, including animals, transports, personal effects, and hazardous items, into and out of a country, while immigration controls and inspects the people entering and leaving the country in order to keep public order of the country. In most cases, passengers will go through customs and immigration after their flight first arrives in a new country, but there are exceptions. For example, some countries have mutual agreements intended to help speed travellers through the process, so they may go through customs and immigration before boarding. And sometimes passengers don't go through customs until they reach their final destination.

In many countries, customs procedures for arriving passengers at many international airports are separated into red and green channels. Passengers with goods to declare (carrying goods above the permitted customs limits and/or carrying prohibited items) go through the red channel, while passengers with nothing to declare (carrying goods within the permitted customs limits and not carrying prohibited items) go through the green channel. False declaration may lead to penalties including confiscation of goods, heavy fines, prosecution, and even imprisonment and/ or removal from that country. Each channel is a point of no return, once a passenger has entered a particular channel, they cannot go back.

Quarantine is a restriction on the movement of people, animals and plants and cargo, which is intended to prevent the spread of diseases or pests. All passengers (nationals and foreigners) entering from another country are subject to health quarantine inspection. When travelling to some countries, especially those in Africa, passengers are requested to show immunization documentation and fill in forms to state that they have got vaccinated against certain contagious disease, like yellow fever, cholera, malaria, etc. During the COVID-19 pandemic, multiple governmental actors enacted quarantines in an effort to curb the rapid spread of the virus. According to the quarantine regulations of many countries, besides valid and approved COVID-19 vaccination certificate and Nucleic Acid Testing Report, passengers may also be requested to fill in a health declaration form, illustrate their latest itineraries and be isolated at home or at designated place for a certain period of time.

In the case of entry with plants, animals or related by-products, passengers must go through Quarantine Inspection and submit the quarantine inspection approval form from the origin country. Without the approval of the quarantine officials; they can't enter into the country. There is usually a list of the items that are not allowed into the country, for example, food including dried, fresh, preserved, cooked and uncooked, plants and their parts, seeds, animals and their parts, animal products, birds, fish, insect, soil and so on. Passengers carrying such items must make a declaration and receive quarantine inspection.

## Decide whether the statements are true or false according to the passage.

1. C.I.Q. regulations in different countries are the same. (    )

2. Immigration is about the people travelling from one country to another while customs is about the stuff those people are carrying with them. (    )

3. Passengers always go through customs and immigration after their flight first arrives in a new country. (    )

4. To prevent the spread of contagious disease and protect the human health, international passengers will be requested to get vaccinated. (    )

5. Countries impose restrictions on the importation of certain plants and animals because these articles may carry infectious diseases. (    )

## Words and Expressions

statement ['steɪtmənt] *n.* 申明

visa ['viːzə] *n.* 签证

disembarkation card 入境卡
tariff [ˈtærɪf] n. 关税
confiscation [ˌkɒnfɪˈskeɪʃn] n. 没收
imprisonment [ɪmˈprɪznmənt] n. 监禁
immunization [ˌɪmjunaɪˈzeɪʃn] n. 免疫
vaccination [ˌvæksɪˈneɪʃn] n. 接种疫苗
pandemic [pænˈdemɪk] n. 流行病
Nucleic Acid Testing Report 核酸检测报告

## 海关起源

英语Customs一词，最早是指商人贩运商品途中缴纳的一种地方税捐，带有"买路钱"或港口、市场"通过费"、"使用费"的性质。

国外最早的海关机构出现在公元前5世纪中叶的古希腊城邦雅典。11世纪以后，西欧威尼斯共和国成立以"海关"命名的机构即威尼斯海关。在漫长的封建社会，各国除继续在沿海、沿边设置海关外，在内地水陆交通要道也设置了许多关卡。资本主义发展前期（17—18世纪），海关执行保护关税政策，重视关税的征收，并建立一套周密烦琐的管理、征税制度。19世纪，为发展对外贸易，欧洲各国先后撤除内地关卡，废止内地关税，并且基本停止出口税的征收。海关历史悠久的发达国家有法国、英国、荷兰、意大利、德国、日本和美国等。发展中国家大部分位于亚洲、非洲和拉丁美洲。这些国家曾经长期遭受殖民主义国家的侵略和剥削，经济比较落后。发展中国家的对外贸易与海关，除向发达国家发展各种方式斗争外，还对该国现代海关制度进行开发和科技运用。

中国海关历史悠久，早在西周和春秋战国时期，古籍中已有关于"关市之征"的记载。秦汉时期进入统一的封建社会，对外贸易发展，西汉元鼎六年（公元前111）在合浦等地设关。宋、元、明时期，先后在广州、泉州等地设立市舶司。清政府宣布开放海禁后，于康熙二十三至二十四年(1684—1685)，首次以"海关"命名，先后设置粤（广州）、闽（福州）、浙（宁波）、江（上海）四海关。1840年鸦片战争后，中国逐渐丧失关税自主权、海关行政管理权和税款收支保管权，海关变成半殖民地性质的海关，长期被英、美、法、日等帝国主义国家控制把持，成为西方列强掠夺中国的一个重要工具。直至1949年中华人民共和国成立以后，人民政府接管海关，宣告受帝国主义控制的半殖民地海关历史结束，标志着社会主义性质海关的诞生。中华人民共和国政府对原海关机构和业务进行彻底变革，经历曲折的发展过程，逐步完善海关建制。

## Text B

## China Customs

In accordance with Customs Law of the People's Republic of China, inward and outward passengers shall enter or leave the territory at the place where the customs is established. Passengers shall be subject to customs control, and shall declare honestly to the customs.

There are two channels set up for passengers to go through customs: "Things-to-declare Channel" (RED CHANNEL) and "Nothing-to-declare Channel" (GREEN CHANNEL). Passengers may choose the appropriate channel in accordance with the Customs regulations. Passengers who "do not understand the customs regulations" or "do not know how to choose the channel" shall go through the "Things-to-declare Channel". No matter which channel the passengers choose, baggage carried by them cannot resist the inspection from the customs.

### Customs Release Criteria

**Caution:** Inward or outward baggage effects, personal articles carried by international passengers shall be limited to the PERSONAL USE only and subject to REASONABLE QUANTITY control. The term "personal use" means private use only or for presenting gifts to relatives or friends, but not for selling or lending. The term "reasonable quantity" means the normal quantities based on the travel purpose and the length of residing time.

**Caution:** Inward passengers with the articles listed below SHALL choose "Goods to Declare" (RED CHANNEL).

| No. | Items |
| --- | --- |
| 1 | Personal articles from overseas, valued at RMB5000 or above, carried by Chinese residents. |
| 2 | Personal articles intended to remain in the territory, valued at RMB2000 or above, carried by non-Chinese residents. |
| 3 | 1500ml or above of alcoholic drinks (containing 12% or above alcoholic content); 400 sticks or above of cigarettes; 100 sticks or above of cigars; 500g or above of tobacco. |
| 4 | RMB20000 cash or above, or any other foreign currencies in cash equivalent to US$5000 or above. |
| 5 | Animals and plants, animal and plant products, microbes, biological products, human tissues, blood and blood products. |
| 6 | Radio transmitters, radio receivers, communication security equipment. |
| 7 | Other articles which are prohibited or restricted from being brought into the territory in accordance with the law of the People's Republic of China. |
| 8 | Goods of commercial value, samples, advertisements. |
| 9 | Unaccompanied baggage. |

**Caution:** Outward passengers with the articles listed below SHALL choose "Goods to Declare" (RED CHANNEL).

| No. | Items |
|---|---|
| 1 | Camera, video camera, laptop computer or other trip necessities valued each at over RMB5000, and intended to be brought back at the end of the trip. |
| 2 | RMB20000 cash or above, or any other foreign currencies in cash equivalent to US$5000 or above. |
| 3 | Gold, silver and other precious metals. |
| 4 | Cultural relics, endangered animals or plants and products thereof, biology species resources. |
| 5 | Radio transmitters, radio receivers, communication security equipment. |
| 6 | Other articles which are prohibited or restricted from being brought out of the territory in accordance with the law of the People's Republic of China. |
| 7 | Goods of commercial value, samples, advertisements. |

## Articles Prohibited from Importation

- Arms, imitation arms, ammunition and explosives of all kinds.
- Counterfeit currencies and counterfeit negotiable securities.
- Printed matter, films, photographs, gramophone records, cinematographic films, loaded recording tapes and video tapes, compact discs ( video and audio ), storage media for computers and other articles which are detrimental to the political, economic, cultural and moral interests of China.
- Deadly poison of all kinds.
- Opium, morphine, heroin, marihuana and other addictive drugs and psychotropic substances.
- Fruits, solanaceae vegetables, live animals (except dogs and cats as pet), animal products, pathogenic micro-organisms of animals and plants, pests and other harmful organisms, animal carcasses, soil, genetically modified organisms, relevant animals and plants, their products and other objects subject to quarantine from countries or regions with prevalent epidemic animal or plant diseases.
- Foodstuff, medicine and other articles coming from epidemic stricken area or harmful to man and livestock or those which might spread disease.

## Articles Prohibited from Exportation:

- All articles enumerated as Articles Prohibited from Importation.
- Manuscripts, printed matter, films, photographs, gramophone records, cinematographic films, loaded recording tapes and video-tapes, compact discs ( video and audio ), storage media for computers and other articles which involve state secrets.
- Valuable cultural relics and other relics prohibited from exportation.
- Endangered and precious rare animals and plants (including their specimens), their seeds and reproducing materials.

## Please answer the following questions according to the passage.

1. What should you do if you are not certain about whether you should declare the items you are carrying at the airport?
2. What is the limitation on the currencies for an inward passenger to carry with him/her?
3. What is the customs duty-free allowance for cigarettes and alcoholic drinks for incoming passengers?
4. Can you list some items that you can't bring into China?
5. Can you list some items that you can't bring out of China besides the articles enumerated as Articles Prohibited from Importation?

## Words and Expressions

territory [ˈterətri] *n.* 领土
currency [ˈkʌrənsi] *n.* 货币
microbe [ˈmaɪkrəʊb] *n.* 微生物
cultural relics 文化遗产
imitation arms 仿真武器
ammunition [ˌæmjuˈnɪʃn] *n.* 弹药
counterfeit [ˈkaʊntəfɪt] *adj.* 伪造的
negotiable securities 有价证券
gramophone records 唱片
compact discs 激光唱片
pathogenic micro-organisms 致病微生物
carcass [ˈkɑ:kəs] *n.* 尸体
epidemic stricken area 疫区

## 客舱服务中的语言技巧

在客舱服务过程中，乘务人员的语言表达绝不能天马行空，想说什么就说什么，用语不当会造成交际障碍，影响客舱服务质量，进而影响公司形象。例如，在某航班中，一位乘务员向乘客询问是否需要点餐，该乘务员对乘客说："是您要饭吗？"结果乘客感到十分恼火，冷冷回道："我要点餐，但我不是要饭的。"在中国文化中"要饭"可表示点餐，但也有乞讨的含义，该乘务员在交流中选词不当，过于随意，某些情况下甚至有贬义，最终造成了交流的失败。客舱服务用语既体现空乘人员个人的水准，又代表着航空公司的精神面貌。可以说语言交际的成败，直接影响着客舱服务的成败。乘务员应根据民航服务业的具体要求和规则说话。其基本原则是：谈吐文雅，清楚明确；用词简洁，通俗活泼；语调亲切平稳；语句流畅，合乎规范；称呼恰当，说话要用尊称；说话方式委婉、热情；语言标准，发音清晰。

随着航空业的发展，不同国家、地域之间的往来交流越来越多，在同一架航班上可能会搭载着不同文化、不同地域、不同种族、不同语言的乘客，空中乘务人员的服务也就有了"跨文化交际"的性质。乘务人员在服务过程中，如果不了解乘客的文化背景，很容易造成与乘客之间的误解，从而导致交际失败，影响服务质量。例如，中国人在迎接远道而来的客人时常常会说"一路辛苦""累了吧"等来表达对对方的关心和礼遇，但如果对欧美乘客直译"You must be very tired."，却会让对方感到反感。在欧美文化中，他们更习惯用"Did you enjoy your trip?"等表达进行问候。再比如，中国人习惯谦虚，在送礼物时常常会说"小东西，不成敬意"。但如果对西方乘客说"Here is a little thing for you. It's not that good."，对方可能会疑惑为什么要送不好的东西。在西方文化中，礼物不在大小贵贱，而在心意，因此，在接受礼物时都会表示热情欣赏的态度。如果在客舱服务中不注意这种文化差异和习惯表达，就很容易造成交流失败，影响客舱服务质量。

## Part Four  Speaking for Communication

**Directions:** Act out the conversations with your partners.

### Conversation A    Filling in the Forms

Conversation A

（CC=Cabin Crew, P=Passenger）

CC: Excuse me, Sir. Would you please fill in the forms before we land?

P1: What are these?

CC: They are Arrival Card, Customs Declaration Form and Quarantine Form.

P1: Do I have to fill them out on board?

CC: You are advised to complete them before landing to speed up your formalities when you go through Customs and Immigration.

P1: OK. Can I write in Chinese?

CC: Sorry, you have to use English and write in capital letters as is instructed here.

P1: I see. I travel with my mum. Does she also have to fill in the forms?

CC: Yes. Every passenger has to fill in the arrival card, while members from the same family can share one form for customs declaration.

P1: Will I give the forms back to you after finishing them?

CC: No. Just keep them with your passport and submit them to the official at the Customs and Immigration.

P1: OK. Thank you.

CC: My pleasure. If you have any difficulties filling out the forms, please turn to any of our crew members.

P1: I will.

P2: Excuse me, Miss.

CC: Yes? Do you need any help, Madam?

P2: My glasses are in my checked luggage. It's quite difficult for me to read these forms. Could you do me a favour?

CC: Certainly. You need to provide some of your detailed information, including your passport number, your family name and given name, date of birth, nationality, country of birth, etc.

P2: Let me see. Here is my passport. You can refer to it.

CC: OK. What's the reason for your trip? And how long are you going to stay there?

P2: I come to New Zealand to attend a conference and I intend to stay there for a week.

CC: OK. And I also need your contact address and mobile phone number.

P2: Wait a moment. I have the address of the hotel on this card. And my phone number is 123456789.

CC: That's done. Do you have items like food, wine or currencies to declare?

P2: I just brought some daily necessities.

CC: OK. Now please sign your name here.

P2: Thank you. That's very kind of you.

CC: It's my duty.

## Words and Expressions

Arrival Card 入境卡

turn to 求助于

checked luggage 托运行李

nationality [ˌnæʃəˈnæləti] *n.* 国籍

conference [ˈkɒnfərəns] *n.* 会议

daily necessities 生活必需品，日用品

## Conversation B　　Questions about Customs and Quarantine

Conversation B

(FA=Flight Attendant, P=Passenger)

P: Excuse me, Miss, could you spare a moment?

FA: Sure. What can I do for you?

P: Actually, this is my first international flight. I've got some questions about the forms for Customs and Quarantine.

FA: What's the problem?

P: I've got a pearl necklace with me. It's a gift for my cousin and I also have the receipt with it. I don't know if I need to declare it.

FA: Well, the duty-free allowance for each gift is CAN$60.

P: Oh, it doesn't cost that much. So I don't think I have to pay the duty. Could you tell me the tax-free limit for cigarettes? I brought 400 cigarettes for my uncle.

FA: I'm afraid you have to declare them. According to the regulation, visitors to Canada can bring 200 cigarettes, 200 tobacco sticks, 50 cigars or cigarillos and 200 grams of manufactured tobacco free of duty for each. And you have to pay duty for the excess.

P: OK. What about the wine? I also bought two bottles of wine at the airport duty-free shop.

FA: That's no problem. I think the customs official will let them pass.

P: Do I have to list all the taxable items including my personal effects?

FA: I'm afraid so. Under the law, failure to properly declare goods, currency and/or monetary instruments brought into Canada may result in seizure action, monetary penalties or even criminal prosecution.

P: I see. I also have a laptop in my carry-on luggage.

FA: Is it also a gift?

P: No. It's just for personal use. And I have used it for many years.

FA: If so, you don't have to declare it.

P: OK. By the way, can I bring apples and sausage into Canada?

FA: I'm afraid not. According to the quarantine regulation of the local government, items including meat and meat products, dairy products, fruits, vegetables, seeds, nuts, plants and animals or their parts and products, cut flowers, soil, wood and wood products, birds and insects must be declared.

P: Oh, what a pity. These sausages are made by my mother as gifts for my relatives.

FA: I'm sorry, but fruits or meat products may carry an infectious virus and spread diseases and pests. To protect the native flora and fauna, these items are prohibited into the country.

P: I understand. What should I do with them?

FA: You can eat some and throw the rest into the garbage can.

P: OK. Thank you so much for your information. You are very considerate.

FA: I am glad I can help. Wish you a nice trip!

## Words and Expressions

allowance [əˈlaʊəns] *n.* 限额
personal effects 个人财产，个人物品
monetary instruments 金融票据
monetary penalties 罚款
prosecution [ˌprɒsɪˈkjuːʃn] *n.* 起诉，诉讼
carry-on luggage 随身携带的行李
infectious [ɪnˈfekʃəs] *adj.* 传染性的

Unit Six　Customs Check（海关检查）

## Part Five   Case Study

案例一：某航班，安全员在执行航班过站期间下机为机组人员购买拉面。后续航班正常登机，旅客登机完毕后带班乘务长未确认安全员是否到位就关闭了舱门，飞机推出滑行时发现安全员未登机，乘务长立刻报告机长，飞机滑回二次开门，航班再遇流控，最终延误等待了近两小时。

事件发生后当班乘务长在部门事件调查处理过程中企图隐瞒事实，阻挠事件调查，推脱责任，坚持自己并不知晓安全员下机一事。后经过核实，安全员下机之前问乘务长索要了客舱任务书，且询问乘务组是否需要带餐食。乘务长的不诚信行为导致有关部门最终加重了对她的处罚。请分析乘务长的做法并提供你的解决方案。

案例二：某空姐多次从国外免税店为亲戚朋友购买化妆品、名牌包并从中赚取一定的辛苦费，且该空姐在携带这些物品入境时未按规定申报，结果在执行某次航班后通过海关入境时被海关人员抽查扣留。最终该空姐被公司解雇并因偷逃税款受到了相应的法律惩处。请分析该空姐的做法并提供你的解决方案。

## Part Six   Further Practice

### Task 1   Writing

**Directions**: Write an announcement that goes before distributing the C.I.Q. cards by using the following words or expressions:

customs, immigration, quarantine, arrival formalities, assist, officials

Announcement

_____
_____
_____
_____
_____

### Task 2   Translating

**Directions:** Translate the following sentences into English.

1. 这是您的海关申报单和入境卡，请用英文大写字母填写，注意与护照一起保存，到达候机楼时可以方便您办理入境手续。

_____

2. 这是入境卡，您可以在落地前填好，落地后交给移民局官员。

_____

3. 美国海关申报单，一个家庭只需填写一份。

_____

4. 根据当地检疫规定，乘客不能携带新鲜水果、肉类、植物以及鲜花等入境。请您在落地前把它们处理掉或交给我们的乘务员。

5. 所有应纳税的项目，例如香烟和酒，都应该在申报表格中列出来，否则会被处很重的罚金。

6. 中国海关规定只允许旅客携带两条香烟入境，您最好不要超过这个限制。

7. 请准备好您的护照、健康证书和疫苗接种证，以便检查。

8. 如果您在填表时遇到任何问题，请随时询问工作人员。我们会随时为您提供帮助。

## Task 3  Story Reading and Retelling

**Directions:** Read the following story in a group and retell it to your group members in your own words.

Once on a domestic flight, the first class was full and five VIP passengers were also seated in this cabin. Thus, the cabin crew worked even more carefully and tried their best to provide the most personalized service to each of them. In the second row seated a foreign passenger who was very easy-going and humorous. He got along well with the flight attendants and made funny faces to them from time to time. This foreign guest has been sleeping since takeoff. When the plane came into smooth flight, flight attendants began serving food and drinks to the passengers and attending to their needs whenever possible.

However, about two hours later, all of a sudden, the foreign passenger rose from his seat and walked straight to the front service desk in a fury. He shouted at the cabin crew in English: "During the two hours of flight, you didn't provide me with any service, not even a cup of water!" Then he returned to his seat again. The cabin crew were very surprised and one of them explained to the purser: "This passenger has been sleeping all the way, so we didn't bother him."

To relieve his anger, the flight attendant brought a cup of water to the passenger but with no doubt was rejected. Then she took some snacks and again was ignored by him. As the plane was about to descend for landing, the flight attendant didn't want him to leave with unpleasant experience. Thus, the flight attendant and her colleagues made a grieved face with fruit. Again, she brought the fruit platter to the passenger and squatted by him and said gently: "Sir, I am very sad! In fact, we have been paying attention to you during flight. After takeoff, you have been sleeping. Then we covered you with a blanket and closed the ventilation holes. We didn't realize you were just resting with eye closed. I should apologize for that." After hearing the explanation, the passenger smiled and said: "You are very sincere. Maybe it is difficult for you to tell whether I am sleeping or just resting. I should also apologize for my rudeness." He then turned the tomato slice upside down, changing the grieved face into a happy and smiley one.

## Task 4  Situational Conversation

**Directions:** The subject matters are given below for several kinds of conversations between the flight attendants or the Customs and Immigration officials and the passengers. Make up short dialogues—four or five lines—that could develop from these situations. Act out the conversation with your partners.

1. When you hand out entry cards, a passenger says he doesn't know English. This is his first flight to a foreign country. He goes to New York to visit his daughter who is studying there. You offer help to him with the forms.

2. A passenger brings some foreign fruits and dairy products, 4 bottles of wine, 6 bars of cigarettes and some medicine with him. You give him some advice when helping him with the Customs Declaration Form.

3. A passenger inquires you about how to go through the Customs and Immigration after landing. You give him instruction patiently.

4. A passenger doesn't feel comfortable with the symptoms of low fever, cough and short breath. You inquire him about his itineraries in the past 14 days and take actions immediately to deal with these abnormal situations.

5. A passenger is going through the Customs and Immigration. He hands in the forms he has completed on board and answers some questions from the officials there.

| Commonly Used English for C.I.Q. | |
|---|---|
| Asking for help | Could you do me a favour? |
| | Excuse me, Miss, could you spare a moment? |
| | Would you mind helping me with these forms? |
| | It's difficult. Can you help? |
| | Could you give me a hand? |
| Positive response to others' request | Sure. What is the problem? |
| | Of course. |
| | With pleasure. |
| | I'll be glad to. |
| Asking for information | Do you know...? |
| | I'd like to know.... |
| | Could you tell me...? |
| | I wonder if you could explain about.... |
| Expressing ideas | I'm afraid you have to pay the duty. |
| | I think the customs official will let them pass. |
| Expressing gratitude | That's very kind of you. |
| | Thank you so much for your information. |
| | You are very considerate. |

| Commonly Used English for C.I.Q. ||
|---|---|
| Expressing being listening | Yes. |
| | Right. |
| | Hmm. |
| Giving advice | You are advised to complete them before landing. |
| | If you have any questions, you can contact any of our crew members. |
| | You'd better…. |
| Customs check | Your passport and declaration card, please. |
| | Do you have anything to declare? |
| | Please bring your bags here for inspection. |
| | Would you please open your bag? |
| | You have to pay duty on this. |
| | How much currency do you have with you? |
| Replies to customs check | I have nothing to declare. |
| | I have a thousand dollar with me. |
| Immigration check | What's the purpose of your visit/stay? |
| | Are you travelling alone? |
| | How long do you intend to stay? |
| | What's your address here? |
| Replies to immigration check | I'm here for school/ business/ vacation. |
| | I'm with a tour group/ my friend/ my family. |
| | I'm here for a week/ for 10 days. |
| Quarantine | Have you brought any food into the country? |
| | Sorry, we don't allow meat from outside of the country. |
| | … is/ are not allowed to be taken into the country. |

# Appendix（附录）

# Appendix 1

## Glossary List
## 词汇表

### A

accessory [əkˈsesəri] *n.* 装饰品，配饰
accidental [ˌæksɪˈdentl] *adj.* 意外的，偶然的
accompany [əˈkʌmpəni] *v.* 陪伴，陪同
administer [ədˈmɪnɪstə(r)] *v.* 实施
aforementioned [əˈfɔːmenʃənd] *adj.* 上述的
ailment [ˈeɪlmənt] *n.* 小病
aircraft [ˈeəkrɑːft] *n.* 飞机
air pressure 气压
airsickness [ˈeəsɪknəs] *n.* 晕机
air security 空中安全
air vent 通风口
airway [ˈeəweɪ] *n.* 呼吸道
aisle [aɪl] *n.* 走廊，过道
allowance [əˈlaʊəns] *n.* 限额
Amiable Angels 亲情使者
ammunition [ˌæmjuˈnɪʃn] *n.* 弹药
apologize [əˈpɒlədʒaɪz] *v.* 道歉
applicable [əˈplɪkəb(ə)l] *adj.* 适用的，适当的
appreciate [əˈpriːʃieɪt] *v.* 感激
approximately [əˈprɒksɪmətli] *adv.* 大约
armrest [ˈɑːmrest] *n.* 扶手
assessment [əˈsesmənt] *n.* 评估
assistance [əˈsɪstəns] *n.* 帮助

assure [əˈʃʊə(r)] v. 保证
attendant [əˈtendənt] n. 服务人员
Arrival Card 入境卡
audio [ˈɔːdiəʊ] adj. 录音的
authorize [ˈɔːθəraɪz] v. 批准，许可
aviation [ˌeɪviˈeɪʃn] n. 航空，航空工业

## B

baggage claim area 行李认领处
belongings [bɪˈlɒŋɪŋz] n. 所有物，行李
beverage [ˈbevərɪdʒ] n. 饮料
blanket [ˈblæŋkɪt] n. 毯子
blow [bləʊ] v. 擤（鼻子）
boarding pass 登机牌
brand [brænd] n. 品牌，商标
Brandy [ˈbrændi] n. 白兰地酒
breathe [briːð] v. 呼吸
briefing [ˈbriːfɪŋ] n. 情况介绍会；简报

## C

cabin [ˈkæbɪn] n. 机舱
cabinet [ˈkæbɪnət] n. 内阁
captain [ˈkæptɪn] n. 机长
carcass [ˈkɑːkəs] n. 尸体
carriage [ˈkærɪdʒ] n. 运输
carry-on luggage 随身携带的行李
category [ˈkætəɡəri] n. 种类；范畴
checked baggage 托运行李
checked luggage 托运行李
checklist [ˈtʃeklɪst] n. 清单；检查表
chew [tʃuː] v. 咀嚼
chute [ʃuːt] n. 瀑布；斜槽；降落伞；陡坡道
cigar [sɪˈɡɑː(r)] n. 雪茄烟
cipher [ˈsaɪfə(r)] n. 密码
circulation [ˌsɜːkjəˈleɪʃn] n. 血液循环
coastal [ˈkəʊst(ə)l] adj. 近海的，沿海的
command [kəˈmɑːnd] n. 命令，指示
commission [kəˈmɪʃn] n. 佣金，回扣
compact discs 激光唱片
compartment [kəmˈpɑːtmənt] n.（飞机、轮船或火车上的）车厢，舱

conference [ˈkɒnfərəns] n. 会议
confiscation [ˌkɒnfɪˈskeɪʃn] n. 没收
connecting flight 转乘航班
conscious [ˈkɒnʃəs] adj. 神志清醒的
consent [kənˈsent] n. 许可，允许
considerate [kənˈsɪdərət] adj. 体贴的，考虑周到的
consign [kənˈsaɪn] v. 托运
consistently [kənˈsɪstəntli] adv. 一贯地，始终
contact [ˈkɒntækt] n. 联系
contractual [kənˈtræktʃuəl] adj. 契约的，合同的
convenience [kənˈviːniəns] n. 方便，便利
conventional [kənˈvenʃənl] adj. 依照惯例的，遵循习俗的；常规的
cosmetics [kɒzˈmetɪks] n. 化妆品
counterfeit [ˈkaʊntəfɪt] adj. 伪造的
cultural relics 文化遗产
cumulus [ˈkjuːmjələs] n. 积云；堆积，堆积物
currency [ˈkʌrənsɪ] n. 通货，货币
Customs Declaration Form 海关申报单

# D

daily necessities 生活必需品，日用品
decline [dɪˈklaɪn] v. 下降，衰退
decompression [ˌdiːkəmˈpreʃn] n. 客舱释压
delegation [ˌdelɪˈgeɪʃn] n. 代表团
denture [ˈdentʃə(r)] n. 假牙
descent [dɪˈsent] n. 下降
designated [ˈdezɪgneɪtɪd] adj. 指定的
destination [ˌdestɪˈneɪʃn] n. 目的地，终点，目标
diagnose [ˌdaɪəgˈnəʊz] v. 诊断（病症）；找出原因
diagnosis proof 诊断证明
diaper [ˈdaɪpə(r)] n. 尿布，纸尿片
diarrhea [ˌdaɪəˈrɪə] n. 腹泻
disarm [dɪsˈɑːm] v. 解除（预位）
disembark [ˌdɪsɪmˈbɑːk] v. 下飞机
disembarkation card 入境卡
dispute [dɪsˈpjuːt] n. 争论，辩论 v. 对……提出质疑，否认；争论
disruption [dɪsˈrʌpʃn] n. 妨碍；扰乱
ditching [ˈdɪtʃɪŋ] n. 水上迫降
dizzy [ˈdɪzi] adj. 眩晕的
domesticated [dəˈmestɪkeɪtɪd] adj. 家养的

drain [dreɪn] *v.* （使）排出，滤干
drop [drɒp] *v.* 投，丢
dual [ˈdjuːəl] *adj.* 双的，双重的
duty-free [ˌdjuːti ˈfriː] *adj.* 免税的 *adv.* 免税地

# E

earache [ˈɪəreɪk] *n.* 耳痛
effective [ɪˈfektɪv] *adj.* 有效的
elastic [ɪˈlæstɪk] *adj.* 有弹性的
emergency landing 紧急迫降
ensure [ɪnˈʃʊə(r)] *v.* 确保
epidemic stricken area 疫区
equipment [ɪˈkwɪpmənt] *n.* 设备
escort [ˈeskɔːt] *v.* 护送
evacuate [ɪˈvækjueɪt] *v.* 疏散，撤离
evacuation [ɪˌvækjuˈeɪʃn] *n.* 撤离，疏散
exceed [ɪkˈsiːd] *v.* 超过，超出
eye shadow 眼影

# F

Frontier Health and Quarantine Law of the People's Republic of China 中华人民共和国国境卫生检疫法
fuselage [ˈfjuːzəlɑːʒ] *n.* 机身（飞机）

# G

give an account of 说明，叙述
Glenfiddich 格兰菲迪（纯麦威士忌）
gramophone records 唱片
guideline [ˈɡaɪdlaɪn] *n.* 指导方针，准则

# H

hail [heɪl] *n.* 冰雹
handle [ˈhændl] *v.* 拿；处理，应付
hesitate [ˈhezɪteɪt] *v.* 犹豫
high-heeled 高跟的
hydrophobic [ˌhaɪdrəˈfəʊbɪk] *adj.* 疏水的，不易被水沾湿的

# I

identification [aɪˌdentɪfɪˈkeɪʃn] *n.* 身份证明

imitation arms 仿真武器
immigration [ˌɪmɪˈɡreɪʃn] *n.* 移民
immunization [ˌɪmjunaɪˈzeɪʃn] *n.* 免疫
imprisonment [ɪmˈprɪznmənt] *n.* 监禁
inadmissible [ˌɪnədˈmɪsəbl] *adj.* 不许可的
in compliance with 按照，遵照
inconvenience [ˌɪnkənˈviːniəns] *n.* 不方便
incur [ɪnˈkɜː(r)] *v.* 招致，带来
infant [ˈɪnfənt] *n.* 婴儿
infectious [ɪnˈfekʃəs] *adj.* 传染性的
inflate [ɪnˈfleɪt] *v.*（使）充气，（使）膨胀
in person 亲自
instruction [ɪnˈstrʌkʃn] *n.* 用法说明，指示
in upright position 处于直立状态
interfere [ˌɪntəˈfɪə(r)] *v.* 干扰
invest [ɪnˈvest] *v.* 投资
issue [ˈɪʃuː] *v.*（正式）发给
item [ˈaɪtəm] *n.* 物品

# J

jewelry [ˈdʒuːəlri] *n.* 珠宝

# L

laptop [ˈlæptɒp] 手提电脑
latch [lætʃ] *v.* 闭锁
latitude [ˈlætɪtjuːd] *n.* 纬度
lavatory [ˈlævətri] *n.* 厕所，盥洗室
liable [ˈlaɪəb(ə)l] *adj.*（在法律上）有责任的
life-threatening [ˈlaɪf θretnɪŋ] *adj.* 威胁生命的
life vest 救生衣
lipstick [ˈlɪpstɪk] *n.* 口红
liquid [ˈlɪkwɪd] *n.* 液体 *adj.* 液态的
liquor [ˈlɪkə(r)] *n.* 烈性酒
logbook [ˈlɒɡbʊk] *n.* 日志

# M

mainland [meɪnlænd] *n.* 大陆
malfunction [ˌmælˈfʌŋkʃn] *n.* 故障，失灵
make a way for sb. 给某人让路

merchandise [ˈmɜːtʃəndaɪs] *n.* 商品，货品
microbe [ˈmaɪkrəʊb] *n.* 微生物
modification [ˌmɒdɪfɪˈkeɪʃn] *n.* 修改
monetary instruments 金融票据
monetary penalties 罚款

# N

nationality [ˌnæʃəˈnæləti] *n.* 国籍
nausea [ˈnɔːziə] *n.* 恶心
navigation system 导航系统
necklace [ˈnekləs] *n.* 项链
negotiable securities 有价证券
Nucleic Acid Testing Report 核酸检测报告

# O

obscure [əbˈskjʊə(r)] *v.* 遮掩，遮蔽
obstructed [əbˈstrʌktɪd] *adj.* 阻塞的
official [əˈfɪʃ(ə)l] *n.* 官员，高级职员
on board 在飞机上
operate [ˈɒpəreɪt] *v.* 操作、运行
overhead compartment 行李架
oxygen [ˈɒksɪdʒən] *n.* 氧气

# P

pandemic [pænˈdemɪk] *n.* 流行病
paralysis [pəˈræləsɪs] *n.* 瘫痪
pathogenic micro-organisms 致病微生物
perfume [ˈpɜːfjuːm] *n.* 香水；芳香
permission [pəˈmɪʃn] *n.* 同意，许可
personal effects 个人财产，个人物品
pilot [ˈpaɪlət] *n.* 飞行员，领航员
placate [pləˈkeɪt] *v.* 安抚
Post-flight Briefing 航后讲评
powdered milk 奶粉
pre-boarding announcement 登机前广播
precipitation [prɪˌsɪpɪˈteɪʃn] *n.* [化学] 沉淀物；降水；冰雹
pregnant [ˈpregnənt] *adj.* 怀孕的
prepare [prɪˈpeə(r)] *v.* 准备
prior [ˈpraɪə(r)] *adj.* 事先的

proceed [prəˈsiːd] v. 开始行动，开展
prohibit [prəˈhɪbɪt] v. 禁止
prosecution [ˌprɒsɪˈkjuːʃn] n. 起诉，诉讼
purchase [ˈpɜːtʃəs] n. 购买
purser [ˈpɜːsə(r)] n. 乘务长，事务长

## Q

quarantine [ˈkwɒrəntiːn] n. 检疫

## R

rash [ræʃ] n. 皮疹
recline [rɪˈklaɪn] v. 向后倾斜
refer to 参考
refraction [rɪˈfrækʃn] n. 折射；折光
regulation [ˌregjuˈleɪʃn] n. 规章制度，规则
release [rɪˈliːs] v. 释放，解开
relieve [rɪˈliːv] v. 缓解（疼痛或不快的感觉）
replace [rɪˈpleɪs] v. 取代，替换
render [ˈrendə(r)] v. 使成为，使处于某种状态；给予
requirement [rɪˈkwaɪəmənt] n. 要求
restrict [rɪˈstrɪkt] v. 限制
rest upon 依赖于，取决于
retract [rɪˈtrækt] v. 缩回；缩进
revenue [ˈrevənjuː] n. 收入，收益；税收
rodent [ˈrəʊdnt] n. 啮齿目动物
rye [raɪ] n. 黑麦

## S

seatbelt [ˈsiːtbelt] n. 座位安全带
selection [sɪˈlekʃ(ə)n] n. 可供选择的东西
shift around 移动，变化
silent review 静默复习
slippery [ˈslɪpəri] adj. 滑的
spinal [ˈspaɪnl] adj. 脊柱的
statement [ˈsteɪtmənt] n. 申明
stow [stəʊ] v. 妥善放置，收好
swallow [ˈswɒləʊ] v. 吞咽
sunglasses [ˈsʌnɡlɑːsɪz] n. 太阳眼镜
suspend [səˈspend] v. 暂停
switch off 关闭

symptom [ˈsɪmptəm] *n*. 症状

# T

take off 起飞
tariff [ˈtærɪf] *n*. 关税
teaspoon [ˈtiːspuːn] *n*. 一茶勺的量
temporary [ˈtemprəri] *adj*. 暂时的
territory [ˈterətri] *n*. 领土
towel [ˈtaʊəl] *n*. 毛巾
trace [treɪs] *v*. 发现，追踪
transit [ˈtrænzɪt] *n*. 运输，运送 *v*. 经过，穿过
turbulence [ˈtɜːbjələns] *n*. 骚乱，动荡；（空气或水的）湍流，紊流
turn to 求助于

# U

unaccompanied [ˌʌnəˈkʌmpənid] *adj*. 无人陪伴（或同行）的
unobstructed [ˌʌnəbˈstrʌktɪd] *adj*. 没有障碍的，畅通无阻的

# V

vacate [vəˈkeɪt; veɪˈkeɪt] *v*. 空出，腾出
vaccination [ˌvæksɪˈneɪʃn] *n*. 接种疫苗
vaccination certificate 检疫证明
vendor [ˈvendə(r)] *n*. 卖方，销售商
ventilation [ˌventɪˈleɪʃn] *n*. 通风
ventilator [ˈventɪleɪtə(r)] *n*. 通风设备
victim [ˈvɪktɪm] *n*. 受害者，患病者
visa [ˈviːzə] *n*. 签证
visibility [ˌvɪzəˈbɪləti] *n*. 能见度
vomit [ˈvɒmɪt] *v*. 呕吐

# W

watch your steps 小心脚下
window blind 遮光帘
window shade 遮光板
wipe [waɪp] *v*. 擦拭

# Appendix 2

## Listening Script
听力原文

## Unit One  Medical Service and First Aid

### Announcement A

#### Introduction to Cabin Equipment and Airsickness

Ladies and gentlemen,

Welcome <u>aboard</u> China Eastern Airlines Flight MU5109 from Shanghaito Beijing. The distance is about 1100 kilometers. Our flight will take two hours and twenty minutes. Breakfast has been prepared for you. We will <u>inform</u> you before we serve it.

Now, I will tell you where the cabin <u>equipment</u> locates and how to use them. Your seat-back can be reclined by pressing the recliner button on your armrest. The reading light, <u>call button</u> and air vent are located above your seat. Airsickness bags are in the seat pocket in front of you.

If you feel like vomiting, please use it. If you are <u>airsick</u> and need some airsick tablets, you can press the call button to <u>contact</u> us.

Lavatories are located in the front and rear of the cabin. <u>Smoking</u> is strictly prohibited on board.

We wish you a <u>pleasant</u> flight.

Thank you!

### Announcement B

#### Searching for a Doctor and Making an Emergency Landing

Ladies and gentlemen,

May I have your <u>attention</u>, please?

We have a passenger <u>giving birth</u> on our aircraft. If you are a <u>doctor or nurse</u>, we would appreciate your assistance by <u>contacting</u> our flight attendants as soon as possible.

Due to the serious condition of the passenger, the captain has decided to make an emergency <u>landing</u> at Beijing Capital International Airport. We expect to arrive there in two hours and twenty-nine minutes.

We <u>apologize</u> for any inconvenience. Thank you for your <u>understanding</u> and <u>cooperation</u>!

# Unit Two  Special Passenger Service

## Announcement A

### Take Care of the Special Passengers

Ladies and gentlemen,

We have just left for Beijing.

During our trip, we shall provide the service of lunch with beverages. We have prepared newspapers for you. This aircraft has audio system; you can use the earphone to choose what you like.

Our captain is a pilot with rich flying experience. As a result, his perfect flying skills will assure you a safe journey. Meanwhile, our "Amiable Angels" in the cabin, who have rich working experience, will take care of the special passengers. To ensure your safety during the flight, we advise you to fasten your seatbelt while seated. If you have any needs or requirements, please let us know.

Wish you a pleasant journey!

Thank you!

## Announcement B

### Pre-boarding Announcement

Ladies and gentlemen,

Good afternoon.

This is the pre-boarding announcement for Flight 4578 to Shanghai. We are now inviting those passengers with small children, and any passengers requiring special assistance, to begin boarding at this time.

Please have your boarding pass and identification ready. Regular boarding will begin in approximately ten minutes.

Thank you.

# Unit Three  Emergency Procedures

## Announcement A

### Emergency Landing/Ditching

Ladies and Gentlemen,

Attention please! It is necessary to make an emergency landing. The crew have been well trained to handle this situation. We will make every effort to ensure your safety keep calm and pay close attention to the flight attendants and follow their instructions.

Please pass your food tray and all other service items for pick up.

Please put the high-heeled shoes, dentures, necklaces, ties, pens, earrings, watches and jewelry in the overhead bin or hand them to the flight attendants.

<u>Fasten</u> your seat belt, bring your seat backs to the upright position and stow all tray tables. Stow footrests and in-seat video units. Please put all of your baggage under the seat in front of you or in the overhead <u>compartment</u>.

(Now the flight attendants will explain the use of life vest. Please put your life vest on and follow the instructions of your flight attendants.)

Now the flight attendants are pointing to the exits nearest to you. Please identify them and be aware your closest <u>exit</u> may be behind you. When <u>evacuating</u>, leave everything on board!

Now we will explain to you brace position against impact. When instructed to brace against impact, put your legs apart, place your feet flat on the floor. <u>Cross</u> your arms like this, lean forward as far as possible, hold the seat back in front of you and rest your face on your arms.

(When instructed to brace against impact, cross your arms above your head, then bend over, keep your head down, and stay down.)

Thank you for your cooperation.

## Announcement B

## Decompression

Ladies and gentlemen, our plane is now being depressurized. Oxygen masks have dropped from the compartment above your seats. Fasten your seat <u>belt</u>; pull a <u>mask</u> sharply toward you and place the mask over your nose and mouth. Pull the elastic <u>band</u> over your head. Remain <u>calm</u> and breathe normally. If you are traveling with a child, attend to yourself first and then to the child. <u>Smoking</u> is not allowed.

# Unit Four  Duty Free Shopping

## Announcement A

## In-flight

Ladies and Gentlemen,

Good afternoon! In order to further meet your traveling <u>needs</u>, we will provide you many local products and international brands. You can <u>select</u> your goods from the duty-free magazine in the seat pocket in front of you. Your cabin attendant is pleased to <u>assist</u> you. All <u>prices</u> are shown in US dollars. Please check <u>with</u> your cabin attendant for prices in other currencies. Most currencies and US dollars, traveler's checks, the major credit cards are accepted for your <u>purchases</u>. Have a good trip!

Thank you.

## Announcement B

### In-flight Duty-free Sales

Ladies and Gentlemen,

We will begin our in-flight duty-free sales <u>service</u> shortly. Our duty-free goods catalogue, with product information, can be <u>found</u> in the seat pocket in front of you. For your convenience, we accept both <u>cash</u> and major international credit cards.

For transit passengers, please note that liquid items purchased <u>onboard</u> are subject to Safety Regulations on Prohibiting Liquid Items onboard. Please feel <u>free</u> to contact any of our flight attendants for more <u>information</u>.

Thank you very much!

## Unit Five  Landing

### Announcement A

### Safety Check and Thanks before Landing

Ladies and gentlemen,

May I have your attention please? Our airplane is expected to arrive in Beijing in approximately 15 minutes. We will be suspending our <u>cabin service</u>. Lavatories have already been suspended. As we start our <u>descent</u>, please make sure your seat backs and <u>tray tables</u> are in their full upright position. Make sure your <u>seat belts</u> are securely fastened and all carry-on luggage is stowed underneath the seat in front of you or in the <u>overhead bins</u>. For passengers sitting by the windows, would you please open the window shades? All personal electronic <u>devices</u> must be turned off, including your laptops and cell phones. We will be <u>dimming</u> the cabin lights for landing.

On behalf of all crew members, we would like to thank you for your support and <u>cooperation</u> during the flight. We hope you enjoy your flight with us!

### Announcement B

### After Landing

Ladies and gentlemen,

We have just arrived at Beijing Capital International Airport. The <u>local time</u> now is 10 a.m.. It is cloudy outside and the temperature is 12 degrees centigrade or 53.6 degrees Fahrenheit. Our airplane is still <u>taxiing</u>. For your safety and comfort, please remain seated and keep your <u>seat belts</u> fastened until the aircraft comes to a full stop and the Fasten-Seat-Belt sign is off. Please take all your belongings when you <u>disembark</u>. Please use caution when opening the overhead compartments, as heavy articles may have shifted around during the flight. Your checked baggage may be <u>claimed</u>

in the baggage claim area. Passengers with connecting flights, please go to transit counter for further information or to check in for your connecting flight in the terminal.

Thank you for choosing our airline and we look forward to serving you again!

# Unit Six   Customs Check

## Announcement A

### Filling out Entry Cards

Ladies and gentlemen, your attention please. Flight CA3205 is going to land at Shanghai Hongqiao International Airport in about 30 minutes. According to the regulations of China, all arriving passengers are required to complete an Entry Card, a Customs Declaration Form and a Quarantine Form. You need to fill out these forms in Chinese or English and keep them with your passport together. Please provide your detailed address in China and sign the forms in person.

Members of the same family should use one Customs Declaration Form. If you are not sure about the items required for declaration, you can refer to the back of the declaration form.

You are advised to complete these forms before reaching our destination in order to shorten the time through the customs and submit them to the officials from the Customs and Immigration on the ground.

If you need any assistance, please don't hesitate to call any of our cabin attendants. Thank you.

## Announcement B

### China Entry Quarantine

Ladies and gentlemen,

May I have your attention please!

In order to protect your health and the health of others, according to the "Frontier Health and Quarantine Law of the People's Republic of China", if you have any symptoms such as fever, cough, breath difficulties, nausea, vomiting, diarrhea, headache, muscle pains, joint pains, rash and so on, please contact our crews as soon as possible, or you might consult the quarantine officials later when arriving.

If you carry with or consign the following articles, such as microbes, human tissues, biological products, blood and blood products, please declare these items to China Inspection and Quarantine and go through the required inspections. Without permissions, you could not carry with or consign the items above.

Insects and animals, which might transmit infectious diseases are not allowed to carry, such as rodents, mosquitoes, cockroaches, etc.

You are welcome to follow this announcement. Any violations will incur the due legal responsibilities. For more information, please inquire the quarantine officials at the airport.

Thank you for your cooperation.

# Answer Keys（参考答案）

# Keys for Unit One

## Part Two

### Announcement A

1. aboard　　2. inform　　3. equipment　　4. call button
5. airsick　　6. contact　　7. Smoking　　8. pleasant

### Announcement B

1. attention　　2. giving birth　　3. doctor or nurse　　4. contacting
5. landing　　6. apologize　　7. understanding　　8. cooperation

## Part Three

### Text A

1. T　　2. F　　3. F　　4. T　　5. F

### Text B

1. C　　2. D　　3. B　　4. D　　5. A

## Part Five

案例一解决方案：

1. 乘务人员第一时间采取急救措施：立即让患者平卧位，取头低脚高位，松开腰带，保暖；保持患者呼吸道通畅；掐患者人中穴或针刺人中、十宣、百会穴；给患者前额冷敷、必要时吸氧、人工呼吸。若患者清醒，让其服用热饮料；

2. 立即通知给机长，广播寻求医疗协助，并尽快转送地面抢救治疗；

3. 经机长同意，可采取记录和乘客签名的方法，了解事件经过或病人附近的两至三名乘客的姓名、家庭住址和电话号码，该乘客应提供身份证或其他有效证件。

案例二解决方案：

1. 乘务人员第一时间采取急救措施：由于机上空间限制，人与人之间距离较近，对病人来说，保证足够的空气流通至关重要，要尽量疏散围观人群，为患者营造一个较为舒适宽敞的环境。就地抢救患者，绝对保持患者安静、平卧，禁止搬运患者；给患者吸氧、吸入亚硝酸异戊酯1支，给予镇静、止痛药物；心跳呼吸骤停时立即开展心肺复苏；

2. 广播寻找医生参加急救，与地面联系做好急救准备；

3. 经机长同意，可采取记录和乘客签名的方法，了解事件经过或病人附近的两至三名乘客的姓名、家庭住址和电话号码，该乘客应提供身份证或其他有效证件。

# Part Six

## Task 1

Examples:

Ladies and gentlemen,

One of our passengers requires medical attention. If you are a doctor or other medical professional, kindly make yourself known to the cabin attendants as soon as possible.

Thank you！

Ladies and gentlemen,

May I have your attention please?

We have a passenger in need of medical attention. If you are a physician or medically trained person, please identify yourself to a flight attendant.

Thank you!

## Task 2

1. Take it easy. This symptom is common.

2. If you feel sick, please use the airsickness bag. It's just located in the seat pocket in front of you.

3. I'm sorry that there's no doctor on board, but we've got in touch with the ground staff at the destination airport.

4. You can just relieve the earache by chewing gums or swallowing.

5. Have you ever felt your heart uncomfortable? Do you bring any medicine with you? Do you have someone traveling with you?

6. This is the medicine for airsickness, and this is a hot towel. I suggest you put it on your head and have a rest. Maybe you will feel better.

7. Keep your arm up. Let's go to wash the cuts. Take it easy. The bleeding is controlled. I'll wrap it up with gauze.

8. The captain has decided to land at the nearest alternate airport.

# Keys for Unit Two

## Part Two

### Announcement A

1. provide
2. newspapers
3. system
4. experience
5. journey
6. special
7. safety
8. needs

### Announcement B

1. afternoon
2. announcement
3. children
4. special
5. boarding pass
6. ten

## Part Three

### Text A

1. A  2. C  3. D  4. A  5. D

### Text B

1. F  2. T  3. T  4. F  5. T

## Part Five

案例一解决方案：

国航规定出生14天以上、身体健康的婴儿，可以搭乘飞机。刚出生没多久的宝宝由于肺部尚未完全张开，毛细血管脆弱，身体对气压、重力等因素变化耐受力较弱，容易被病菌感染。如果让宝宝跟一大群陌生人在封闭环境中共同呼吸循环使用的空气，难免会被一些流窜的病菌感染。如果出现了身体不舒服的症状，需要及时去医院就诊。因此，妈妈们最好等到宝宝4～6周以后再带着宝宝坐飞机。

案例二解决方案：

小旅客上飞机时，乘务员在征得小旅客同意后牵着她的手，带她入座，亲切地向小旅客介绍飞机的设施。飞机平飞后，乘务员见小旅客仍然很拘束，便将飞机上的折纸拿出来，用心地折了几个小动物送给她。当小旅客看到玩具折纸时，选了自己最喜欢的折纸小动物玩起来，并叫乘务员教她一起折，开心地笑了。

乘务员一路上主动询问小旅客喝不喝水，给予她密切关注。小旅客下飞机前，乘务员帮她整理好书包，小旅客依依不舍地和乘务员道别。

# Part Six

## Task 1

Examples:

Ladies and gentlemen,

Good morning! Welcome aboard Shanghai Airlines' flight from Shanghai to Beijing. I am the purser of this flight. We're glad to fly with you and would like to be at your service. Our flight attendants in the cabin have a lot of working experience, and will take care of the special passengers.

Thank you!

Ladies and gentlemen,

Good afternoon! We have just left for Shanghai.

I am Mary, your purser. First I represent the China Southern Airlines to extend my most sincere greeting to you. Our crew members who have rich working experience will do our best to provide service for the special passengers.

Thank you!

## Task 2

1. If you want to change the baby diaper, you can go to the lavatory.

2. If you need any help, please press the call button above your head to let me know.

3. The lavatory is located in the front and rear of the cabin.

4. Let me help you with your baggage/luggage.

5. Madam, this is the blanket for you.

6. You have to change the special wheelchair on board.

7. May I help you put your small backpack into the overhead compartment?

8. I'm afraid the guide dog can't take a passenger seat.

# Keys for Unit Three

## Part Two

### Announcement A

1. emergency   2. crew   3. instructions   4. Fasten
5. compartment   6. exit   7. evacuating   8. Cross

### Announcement B

1. belt   2. mask   3. band   4. calm   5. Smoking

## Part Three

### Text A

1. In the case of a small aircraft, it is recommended that pilots carry a set of emergency procedure checklists readily available to them in the event of an emergency. Emergency procedures cover a variety of topics dealing with engine failures, in-flight fires, electrical failures, flight control malfunctions and others.

2. In larger transport aircraft, more than one pilot is available to assist during crisis situations, and the delegation of responsibility at such times rests upon the pilot in command.

3. In modern aircraft with electronic flight instrumentation there are often systems onboard the aircraft that will assist the flight crew in diagnosing a problem and will provide the appropriate checklist. This display highlights the appropriate checklist items and forces the crew to acknowledge each checklist item before proceeding to the next item.

4. Research has shown that those passengers who listen to the preflight emergency briefing information are much more likely to survive an air accident than those who do not.

### Text B

1. F   2. F   3. T   4. T   5. T

## Part Five

案例一解决方案：

1. 尽管旅客第一时间不是质疑我们的服务出了什么问题，但是毕竟我们是第一个听到旅客抱怨的人，而我们做出的任何反应可以直接影响到旅客接下来的态度和决定。我们也许该更深入的思考、分析一下，为什么？没有无缘无故的抱怨和指责。也许旅客此刻正处于一种不安、紧张、恐惧的状况，那么旅客需要的不是解释，而是安抚，例如："很抱歉给您造成了不便，今天确实是因为……（说明原因），请不要担心"；

2. 在面对旅客时，服务人员即代表航空公司，应有大局意识，在回答问题时，严禁推卸责任，例如可以说："很抱歉造成了您的困扰，我一定给您反映……谢谢您的宝贵意见"；

3. 积极地回应，注意为旅客提供多种选择，例如可以说："我马上去看看是什么原因好吗？或者您看要不这样好吗？……"。

案例二解决方案：

航空公司应该尽量减少飞机的延误，加大航班正常的管理力度，抓住航班运行的关键控制点和薄弱环节，细化保障措施。当飞机延误时要耐心地向乘客解释并提供必要的服务。像上述案例空乘人员没有尽早发现问题，在飞机不得不延误飞行时没有及时给乘客解释和提供好的服务，有可能导致个别乘客拒绝乘机或者是占机不下，不仅影响民用航班秩序和航空运输安全，也会损害后续航班旅客的权益，更对空乘服务质量有严重影响。

# Part Six

## Task 1

Example:

## Fire Extinguished

Ladies and gentlemen,

The fire has been completely put out. The plane is cruising as scheduled to London. Thank you for your assistance and cooperation.

Thank you！

## Task 2

1. Because the plane meets severe turbulence, please fasten your seat belts at once.

2. Bend down and place your head between your knees, then grab your knees.

3. Bring seat backs to the upright position and stow all tray tables, straight up your footrest.

4. The lavatories have been closed because the plane is encountering severe turbulence.

5. Don't be worried. Please keep calm. Our captain has full competence and confidence to land the plane safely.

6. There is a possibility that our plane will stay overnight at this alternate airport.

7. The plane will make an emergency landing due to the oil leakage.

8. You aren't allowed to release your seat belts until the plane comes to a complete stop.

# Keys for Unit Four

## Part Two

### Announcement A

1. needs   2. select   3. assist
4. prices  5. with     6. purchases

### Announcement B

1. service  2. found   3. cash
4. onboard  5. free    6. information

## Part Three

### Text A

1. F   2. F   3. T   4. F   5. T

### Text B

1. American Airlines has stopped selling duty-free merchandise on select international flight due to a contractual disagreement between American Airlines and DFASS.

2. Because he or she considered it more of a disruption than a benefit.

3. Duty-free in-flight sales have been declining over the past decade because of the increase in duty-free stores at airports as well as the greater availability of goods on the Internet.

4. Duty-free shopping can be traced back to the 1940s when Brendan O'Regan opened up a duty-free shop that sold Irish goods to passengers on a refueling stop at Rineanna (now Shannon) Airport.

5. The Delta purser feels happy to hear the news.

## Part Five

案例一解决方案：

相关专家表示免税店是向规定的对象销售、供应免税品的商店。在中国境内设立的免税店，除了在关税适用规则上不同外，同样应遵守国内的法律规则，并无特殊之处。免税商品无特殊性，也不是特权商品。免税店也应同样遵守《产品质量法》、《消费者权益保护法》等法律规定。对于免税店中销售的商品，如消费者认为其产品质量存在问题，有权依据法律规定向免税店提出享受"三包"政策待遇，免税店应当予以配合处理。

案例二解决方案：

此类事件发生，应先清点完总收入后再答复旅客，未经清点，自己掏钱给旅客的做法是欠妥，且容易产生更大的误解。此类案件的发生，反映出机上售卖模式对通常购物时采取的一手交钱一手交货、人们普遍认同并接受的交易模式的挑战。在乘客质疑少找钱的情况下，乘务员应该回应："先生/女士请您稍等，我先清点一下总账，看是否忘记找您钱。"清点完之后发现总账是对的，并没有少找，再恳请乘客清点一下自己的美金总数。整个过程中，乘务员应保持冷静，态度亲切，并努力帮助乘客解决问题。

## Part Six

### Task 1

Examples:

Ladies and gentlemen,

Good morning! Continental Airlines introduces another special service for you on this flight: a unique shopping experience while flying.

Within the pages of the newest Continental Collection, you will discover an unparalleled collection of over 60 items from the world's most sought-after names: jewelry from Misaki, Carolee and Swarovski, watches from Anne Klein and Kenneth Cole, toys, liquor, fragrances and cosmetics, all available to purchase duty-free while on board and to take with you.

Look for a copy of the Continental Collection catalog in the seat pocket on board. Your flight attendant will be pleased to assist you with your selection.

All prices are in U.S. dollars. Most major currencies, traveler's checks and credit cards are accepted.

Enjoy your shopping and flight.

Thank you!

### Task 2

1. In order to meet your traveling needs, we will provide you all kinds of duty free goods.

2. If you want to know the price of other currencies, please consult your cabin attendant.

3. All the items provided on board are at market prices.

4. I'm sorry we don't accept checks. You can only pay in cash or by credit card.

5. Hello, Sir. What kind of duty-free goods do you want to buy?

6. This cosmetic is too expensive. Can you give me a discount?

7. The duty-free brochure is in the seat pocket in front of you. You may have a look at it first.

8. Excuse me, Miss. Do you sell duty-free items in the cabin?

# Keys for Unit Five

## Part Two

### Announcement A

| | | | |
|---|---|---|---|
| 1. cabin service | 2. descent | 3. tray tables | 4. seat belts |
| 5. overhead bins | 6. devices | 7. dimming | 8. cooperation |

### Announcement B

| | | | |
|---|---|---|---|
| 1. local time | 2. taxiing | 3. seat belts | 4. disembark |
| 5. claimed | 6. connecting flights | 7. transit counter | 8. terminal |

## Part Three

### Text A

1. F  2. F  3. T  4. F  5. T

### Text B

1. Post-flight brief is the final stage of the flight attendants' work in the flight.

2. Usually post-flight briefings tend to be less formal and shorter in duration than pre-flight briefings.

3. The cabin crew will discuss all onboard situations and issues, including service to special categories of passengers such as infants, unaccompanied children, persons with disabilities, inadmissible passengers and so on, resolving passengers' complaints due to missed drinks, wrong meals, turbulent conditions, minor ailments etc., emergencies and how they are handled during flight, passengers' advice and suggestions as well as other typical issues.

4. For the crew members who made mistakes, the purser may give advice on improvement or report to his superior leader if necessary. And the assessment results will be recorded in the cabin crew logbook.

5. It is beneficial for both the airline and cabin crew. Debriefing is important to identify things that went wrong or not as planned during the flight: any issues or emergencies, as well as planned and unplanned decisions, based on which the airline and the cabin crew can make adjustments in order to provide better service to its passengers in the future.

# Part Five

案例一解决方案：

1. 当安全与服务发生冲突时，乘务员应当使用良好的沟通技巧来化解旅客心中的疑惑，要学会揣摩旅客的心情，并从言语中去告知旅客，安全的执行更多是为保护其自身的安全，乘务员也是秉承对旅客的安全负责；

2. 面对不经常乘机的旅客，乘务员更应耐心、细心地向旅客解释空中的规定，设身处地从旅客角度去分析并解决问题；

3. 建议话语："女士，很抱歉现在飞机下降了，真的不忍心打扰您和宝宝，但恐怕您还是要叫醒他并系好安全带。您是不是感到耳膜受到挤压？更何况小孩的耳朵更敏感。如果下降的时候不叫醒他并让他做一些吞咽动作，对他的耳膜会造成伤害。我们建议您让他坐着，因为孩子躺着会伤到脊椎，如果您想抱着他的话，我们需要给您提供婴儿安全带，但是宝宝超过两周岁了吧，婴儿安全带扣不上了。下降阶段难免会遇到一些颠簸，我们更建议您让他单独坐，所以为了将不安全因素降到最低，还是把孩子叫醒、坐好并系好安全带吧。"

案例二解决方案：

1. 乘务员在按规定执行任务的同时应灵活掌握原则。当刚播送完飞机下降广播时的10分钟内可以灵活掌控，让旅客使用洗手间，但同时善意提醒旅客飞机下降过程中可能有颠簸，请扶好，同时委婉提醒旅客飞机已开始下降，请稍快一些。

2. 手册要求离飞机落地10分钟所有乘务员应坐好，并系好安全带。此时如果有旅客要求使用洗手间应婉言阻止，告知其危害性。

3. 最后，乘务员应注意在要求旅客的同时，自己应该首先以身作则。

# Part Six

## Task 1

Examples:

### Before Landing

Ladies and gentlemen,

We are expected to arrive at the destination airport in about 15 minutes. Please be seated and fasten your seat belt. Please raise your seat backs and tray tables to the full upright and locked position. All personal computers and cell phones should be switched off. Please ensure that all carry-on items are completely under the seat in front of you or in the overhead compartments, leaving the area around your feet clear. We will come by one last time to pick up cups, cans, newspapers, and any other trash. Thank you for your cooperation.

Thank you！

## Task 2

1. Our plane will be landing shortly. For your safety, please remain seated with your seat belt fastened until the Captain turns off the Fasten Seat Belt sign.

2. Thank you for flying with us and we look forward to having the opportunity to meet with you again.

3. We kindly remind you to take care of your small items especially during landing.

4. We are about to turn off the cabin light. If you would like to read, we suggest you use your reading light.

5. Transit passengers please proceed to the departure hall in the terminal building to arrange your connecting flight.

6. We sincerely apologize for the flight delay and thank you for your understanding and cooperation.

7. Please take all your belongings with you when disembarking.

8. Your checked luggage may be claimed at the luggage claim area at the arrival hall.

# Keys for Unit Six

## Part Two

### Announcement A

1. regulations   2. Entry Card   3. passport   4. address
5. items         6. back         7. submit     8. hesitate

### Announcement B

1. breath difficulties   2. headache   3. contact   4. consult   5. declare
6. inspections   7. infectious diseases   8. legal responsibilities

## Part Three

### Text A

1. F   2. T   3. F   4. F   5. T

## Text B

1. Passengers who are not certain about the declared items shall ask the Customs officers for details or choose the "Goods to Declare Channel" (RED CHANNEL).

2. RMB20,000 cash, or any other foreign currencies in cash equivalent to US$5,000.

3. 1,500ml alcoholic drinks (containing 12% or above alcoholic content); 400 sticks of cigarettes; 100 sticks cigars; 500g tobacco.

4. Fruits, solanaceae vegetables, live animals (except dogs and cats as pet), animal products, pathogenic micro-organisms of animals and plants, pests and other harmful organisms, animal carcasses, soil, genetically modified organisms, relevant animals and plants, their products and other objects subject to quarantine from countries or regions with prevalent epidemic animal or plant diseases....(refer to the Articles Prohibited from Importation)

5. Valuable cultural relics and other relics prohibited from Exportation. Endangered and precious rare animals and plants (including their specimens), their seeds and reproducing materials... (refer to the Articles Prohibited from Exportation)

## Part Five

案例一 解决方案：

1. 带班人员未担负好关机门前管理职责，没有在关机门前确认所有人员登机（包括机组人员、安全员）便盲目关门，导致安全员未到位就关闭舱门，造成飞机滑回的运行差错。"客舱服务手册"的关机门前管理中明确要求客舱经理/乘务长应确认飞行机组、客舱机组、安全员、跟班机务等所有成员已到齐，无关人员已下机方可报告机长，请示关门。

2. 带班人员应时刻明确"岗位禁令"，禁止过站期间客舱机组人员及安全员下飞机做与当天飞行任务无关的事，乘务员要对岗位禁令有一份敬畏之心。

3. 事件发生后带班人员的不诚信行为暴露出了其在个人品德、职业道德上存在严重缺失，不真诚对待组织，没有正确的从业观，企图逃避责任，这种错误的侥幸心理害人害己。所有机组人员应加强学习"四德"教育，做人的基本准则是诚信为本，航班飞行更应如此。

案例二 解决方案：

1. 国际航班抵达之后，无论是乘客还是机组人员，一般入境的时候都有两条通道，一条是无申报通道，一条是有申报通道。根据中国海关的现行规定，进境居民旅客携带在境外获取的自用物品，总值在5000元人民币(含5000元)以内的，海关予以免税放行，超出的部分应按海关核定的完税价格和相应税率缴税。通常对于绝大部分乘客和机组人员来说，他们都是走无申报通道入境的，所以都将面临海关工作人员的抽查，来检验旅客的行李中是否有违规携带货。在执行国际航班前，乘务人员应认真学习有关出入境的法律法规，不应抱有侥幸心理，触犯法律。

2. 航空公司对于乘务人员代购有着十分严格的规定：出入境机组仅可携带旅途必需和零星自用物品，严禁违法违规的捎、买、带行为，不得利用执行航班任务从事以营利为目的的生产经营活动；航司允许乘务员携带适量生活用品及化妆品，但须以旅途必须以个人自用为前提，且均需按海关相关法律规定携带。如有航空公司发现乘务员大规模代购，最高可以处以停飞处罚。因此，乘务人员应严守底线，遵守公司规定，加强纪律意识，不踩"红线"。

# Part Six

## Task 1

Examples:

### CIQ Card Distribution

Ladies and gentlemen,

May I have your attention please?

We will be distributing the forms for customs, immigration and quarantine which you need to fill out before landing in order to speed up your arrival formalities in the airport. If you have any problems filling in the form, please feel free to let us know and we will be glad to assist you.

After landing, please hand the completed forms to the officials of the Customs and Immigration Authority.

Thank you for your cooperation.

## Task 2

1. Here are the Customs Declaration Form and Entry Card. Please fill out the forms using capital letters and keep them with your passport together. It'll be convenient for you to go through the entry formalities in the terminal building.

2. Here is the entry card. You may fill it out before landing and submit it to the official when going through immigration.

3. For the customs declaration form of the United States, only one form is necessary for a family traveling together.

4. According to the quarantine regulations of the local government, passengers are not allowed to bring fresh fruits, meat, vegetation or flowers, etc. into the country. Please dispose of them or give them to the flight attendants before landing.

5. All taxable items such as cigarettes and wine should be listed on the Customs Declaration Form. Otherwise, you will be subject to heavy fine.

6. Chinese Customs permits 2 cartons of cigarettes into the country, so you'd better not exceed the limit.

7. Please get your passport, health certificate and vaccination certificate ready for inspection.

8. Please feel free to contact us if you have any problems filling out this form. We are glad to be at your service.

# References(参考文献)

1. What is a Flight Attendant?
https://www.wise-geek.com/what-is-a-flight-attendant.htm
2. In-flight Medical Emergency: an Overview
http://www.360doc.com/content/19/0219/11/675649_816049375.shtml
3. How to Become a Flight Attendant?
https://www.howtobecome.com/how-to-become-a-flight-attendant
4. Notice for Senior Passengers
https://global.tianjin-air.com/CN/GB/travel-preparation/care-more/senior-passengers
5. Passengers with Children
https://eng.tolmachevo.ru/passengers/rules/children/
6. Baby on Board
https://m.kekenet.com/menu/201706/512837.shtml
7. http://www.chinadaily.com.cn
8. http://www.frequentbusinesstraveler.com
9. http://www.tup.com.cn
10. Cabin Crew Manual，Air China，2013.
11. In-flight Passenger Announcements
https://airodyssey.net/reference/inflight
12. https://scottscheapflights.com/glossary/customs-and-immigration
13. https://en.wikipedia.org/wiki/Customs
14. http://english.customs.gov.cn/
15. https://baike.baidu.com/item
16. In-flight Announcement Manual, China Eastern Airlines, 2014.
17. 范晔，邹海欧. 空中乘务情景英语. 北京：清华大学出版社，2018.
18. 高锋，齐超. 航空乘务英语教程. 上海：同济大学出版社，2013.